T0383728

Information Disorder

This book focuses on the recent rise of "infodemics" as forms of disinformation, misinformation and mal-information saturate contemporary media platforms, shaping public opinion to advance agendas.

The internet in general and social media in particular have relativized, through their global, complex and instantaneous information flows, assumptions about truth and authority in fact-based content. This has created new opportunities for state actors to use information beyond traditional conceptions of propaganda to directly assault a public's conception of reality. Additionally, almost anyone has the capability to challenge evidential claims through narratives and imagery alone as there is a wide appetite online for alternative realities. This requires new approaches to media literacy in education, the creative arts and our acts of media consumption and dissemination. The volume covers the ways that social media platforms amplify and catalyze the messages of politicians and influencers, the ambivalence of algorithms that can both generate and detect problematic information, how fake news imitates the style of memes to gain widespread social traction and virality, and how artists have intentionally created "sicko AIs" in new media performances to highlight the ethical risks of increasingly "intelligent" technologies.

Scholars and students from many backgrounds, as well as policy makers, journalists and the general reading public, will find a multidisciplinary approach to questions posed by information disorder research from the fields of communication, social psychology, human-computer interaction, journalism, media, semiotics and new media art.

Michael Filimowicz is Senior Lecturer in the School of Interactive Arts and Technology (SIAT) at Simon Fraser University. He has a background in computer-mediated communications, audiovisual production, new media art and creative writing. His research develops new multimodal display technologies and forms, exploring novel form factors across different application contexts including gaming, immersive exhibitions and simulations.

Algorithms and Society
Series Editor
Dr Michael Filimowicz
Senior Lecturer in the School of Interactive Arts and Technology (SIAT) at Simon Fraser University.

As algorithms and data flows increasingly penetrate every aspect of our lives, it is imperative to develop sufficient theoretical lenses and design approaches to humanize our informatic devices and environments. At stake are the human dimensions of society which stand to lose ground to calculative efficiencies and performance, whether at the service of government, capital, criminal networks, or even a general mob concatenated in social media.

Algorithms and Society is a new series which takes a broad view of the information age. Each volume focuses on an important thematic area, from new fields such as software studies and critical code studies to more established areas of inquiry such as philosophy of technology and science and technology studies. This series aims to stay abreast of new areas of controversy and social issues as they emerge with the development of new technologies.

If you wish to submit a book proposal for the series, please contact Dr Michael Filimowicz michael_f@sfu.ca or Emily Briggs emily.briggs@tandf.co.uk

Algorithmic Ethics
Algorithms and Society
Edited by Michael Filimowicz

China's Digital Civilization
Algorithms and Society
Edited by Michael Filimowicz

Decolonizing Data
Algorithms and Society
Edited by Michael Filimowicz

Information Disorder
Algorithms and Society
Edited by Michael Filimowicz

For more information on the series, visit: www.routledge.com/Algorithms-and-Society/book-series/ALGRAS

Information Disorder

Algorithms and Society

Edited by Michael Filimowicz

Routledge
Taylor & Francis Group

LONDON AND NEW YORK

First published 2023
by Routledge
4 Park Square, Milton Park, Abingdon, Oxon OX14 4RN

and by Routledge
605 Third Avenue, New York, NY 10158

Routledge is an imprint of the Taylor & Francis Group, an informa business

British Library Cataloguing-in-Publication Data
A catalogue record for this book is available from the British Library

Library of Congress Cataloging-in-Publication Data
Names: Filimowicz, Michael, editor.
Title: Information disorder : algorithms and society / edited by
    Michael Filimowicz.
Description: Abingdon, Oxon ; New York, NY : Routledge, 2023. |
    Series: Algorithms and society | Includes bibliographical references
    and index.
Identifiers: LCCN 2023009415 (print) | LCCN 2023009416 (ebook) |
    ISBN 9781032290775 (hardback) | ISBN 9781032290782 (paperback) |
    ISBN 9781003299936 (ebook)
Subjects: LCSH: Social media—Moral and ethical aspects. | Misinformation. |
    Disinformation. | Public opinion.
Classification: LCC HM741 .I545 2023 (print) | LCC HM741 (ebook) | DDC
    302.23/1—dc23/eng/20230413
LC record available at https://lccn.loc.gov/2023009415
LC ebook record available at https://lccn.loc.gov/2023009416

ISBN: 978-1-032-29077-5 (hbk)
ISBN: 978-1-032-29078-2 (pbk)
ISBN: 978-1-003-29993-6 (ebk)

DOI: 10.4324/9781003299936

Typeset in Times New Roman
by Apex CoVantage, LLC

Contents

Figures

Tables

Contributors

Tatiana Hidalgo-Marí is Senior Lecturer in the Department of Communication and Social Psychology at the University of Alicante (UA). She holds a doctorate in audiovisual communication and advertising (2013), a master's in communication and creative industry (2012) and a bachelor's in advertising and PR (2007); she is also Professor of Semiotics of Mass Communication and Semiotics of Advertising in the Degree in Advertising and Public Relations at the UA.

Chenyan Jia (Ph.D., The University of Texas at Austin) is a postdoctoral scholar in the Program on Democracy and the Internet (PDI) at Stanford University. Her research interests lie at the intersection of communication and human-computer interaction.

Taeyoung Lee (M.A., Indiana University) is a doctoral candidate in the School of Journalism and Media at the University of Texas at Austin. Her research focuses on mediated political communication with a specific focus on mis- and disinformation.

Sara Monaci is Associate Professor in Media and Communication at Politecnico di Torino, (DIST). She's Delegate of the Rector for Cinema and Media Engineering (bachelor and master degree). She teaches multimedia communication, future storytelling, information and communication technologies (ICT), communication and society in the course of degree in cinema and media engineering (Politecnico di Torino), and she's a member of the International Research Network Sociology of Culture for European Sociological Association (ESA). In the past years she was visiting scholar at the London School of Economics, UK (2018) and Brown University, US (2007). Her research interests involve internet studies, digital media and political extremism, social media and misinformation/fake news and storytelling. Among her latest publications: Monaci, S. (2021), The Pandemic of Conspiracies in the COVID-19 Age: How Twitter Reinforces Online Infodemic, *Online Journal of Communication and Media Technologies*, M. Bastas Publishing, pp. 11, Vol. 11, ISSN: 1986–3497, DOI: 10.30935/

ojcmt/11203; Monaci, S. (2020). "The Propaganda Machine: Social Media Bias and the Future of Democracy," In: *Reimagining Communication: Meaning*, pp. 233–247, Routledge; Monaci, S.(2020). Social Media Campaigns Against Violent Extremism: A New Approach to Evaluating Video Storytelling. *International Journal of Communication*, 14, 24.

Ellen Pearlman is a New York–based new media artist, curator, critic and educator. A Fulbright Scholar at the Department of Mathematics at the University of Warsaw, Poland, she has also been a Fulbright Specialist in New Media, Art and Technology in Latvia and Poland. A Research Fellow at MIT, she is also Senior Research Assistant Professor at RISEBA University in Riga, Latvia. Ellen has been a Zero1 American Arts Incubator/ US State Department Artist to Kyiv, Ukraine, and a Vertigo STARTS Laureate (EU). She received her doctorate from the School of Creative Media, Hong Kong City University, where her Ph.D. thesis received Highest Global Honors from Leonardo LABS Abstracts. Ellen is also the founder and director of ThoughtWorks Arts, a global technology research lab. She created "Noor: A Brainwave Opera" and "AIBO—An Emotionally Intelligent Artificial Intelligence Brainwave Opera." Currently, she is working on "Language Is Leaving Me, An Opera of the Skin," which explores AI, computer vision and epigenetic trauma of cultures of diaspora.

Raúl Rodríguez-Ferrándiz is Full Professor of Semiotics of Mass Communication and Transmedia Production at the University of Alicante, Spain. He has been academic coordinator of the Master of Communication and Creative Industries at the same university. He has published the books *Magics of Fiction: Spoiler Warning!* (International Essay Prize "Miguel de Unamuno," Bilbao, 2019, Madrid, Devenir, 2020); *Masks of Lying: The New Post-Truth Disorder* (XXXV International Essay Prize "Ciudad de Valencia," 2017; Valencia, Pre-Textos, 2018); *The Venal Muse: Production and Consumption of Industrial Culture* (International Essay Prize "Miguel Espinosa," Murcia, Tres Fronteras, 2010); and *Apocalypse Show: Intellectuals, TV and End of the Millennium* (Madrid, Biblioteca Nueva, 2001). He has coordinated the volume *The Controversy on Mass Culture in the Inter-War Period: A Critical Anthology* (University of Valencia, 2012).

Cande Sánchez-Olmos is Senior Lecturer in the Department of Communication and Social Psychology at the University of Alicante in Spain, where she teaches the course Semiotics of Mass Media and Transmedia Production at the Communication and Creative Industries postgraduate degree. She is author/coauthor of numerous articles and book chapters about transmedia, participatory culture, memetics, brand placement, music, advertising and music videos. She is visiting researcher at Goldsmiths, University of London (Department of Media, Communication and Cultural Studies during 2022–2023), and she was visiting researcher at the City University of London (2013) and Glasgow Caledonian University (2017). Her Ph.D. was awarded by the University of Alicante in 2019, and she won the Prat Gaballí national research award in advertising in 2009. Besides, she accounts 12 years of professional experience working in media, communication and cultural management in Spain.

Series Preface

Algorithms and Society

Michael Filimowicz

This series is less about what algorithms are and more about how they act in the world through "eventful" (Bucher, 2018, p. 48) forms of "automated decision making" (Noble, 2018, loc. 141) in which computational models are "based on choices made by fallible human beings" (O'Neil, 2016, loc. 126).

> Decisions that used to be based on human refection are now made automatically. Software encodes thousands of rules and instructions computed in a fraction of a second.
>
> (Pasquale, 2015, loc. 189)

> If, in the industrial era, the promise of automation was to displace manual labor, in the information age it is to pre-empt agency, spontaneity, and risk: to map out possible futures before they hap-pen so objectionable ones can be foreclosed and desirable ones selected.
>
> (Andrejevic, 2020, p. 8)

> [M]achine learning algorithms that anticipate our future propensities are seriously threatening the chances that we have to make possible alternative political futures.
>
> (Amoore, 2020, p. xi)

Algorithms, definable pragmatically as "a method for solving a problem" (Finn, 2017, loc. 408), "leap from one feld to the next" (O'Neil, 2016, loc. 525). They are "hyperobjects: things with such broad temporal and spatial reach that they exceed the phenomenological horizon of human subjects" (Hong, 2020, p. 30). While in the main, the techno-logical systems taken up as volume topics are design solutions to problems for which there are commercial markets, organized communities, or claims of state interest, their power and ubiquity generate new problems for inquiry. The series will do its part to track this domain fuidity across its volumes and contest, through critique and investigation, their "logic of secrecy" (Pasquale, 2015, loc. 68), and "obfuscation" (loc. 144).

These new social (rather than strictly computational) problems that are generated can, in turn, be taken up by many critical, policy, and speculative discourses. At their most productive, such debates can potentially alter the ethical, legal, and even imaginative parameters of the environments in which the algorithms of our information architectures and infrastructures operate, as algorithmic implementations often reflect a "desire for epistemic purity, of knowledge stripped of uncertainty and human guesswork" (Hong, 2020, p. 20). The series aims to foster a general intervention in the conversation around these often "black boxed" technologies and track their pervasive effects in society.

> Contemporary algorithms are not so much transgressing settled societal norms as establishing new patterns of good and bad, new thresholds of normality and abnormality, against which actions are calibrated.
>
> (Amoore, 2020, p. 5)

Less "hot button" algorithmic topics are also of interest to the series, such as their use in the civil sphere by citizen scientists, activists, and hobbyists, where there is usually not as much discursive attention. Beyond private, state, and civil interests, the increasingly sophisticated technology-based activities of criminals, whether amateur or highly organized, deserve broader attention as now everyone must defend their digital identities. The information systems of companies and states conduct a general form of "ambient surveillance" (Pasquale, 2015, loc. 310), and anyone can be a target of a hacking operation.

Algorithms and Society thus aims to be an interdisciplinary series which is open to researchers from a broad range of academic back-grounds. While each volume has its defined scope, chapter contributions may come from many areas such as sociology, communications, critical legal studies, criminology, digital humanities, economics, computer science, geography, computational media and design, philosophy of technology, and anthropology, along with others. Algorithms are "shaping the conditions of everyday life" (Bucher, 2018, p. 158) and operate "at the intersection of computational space, cultural systems, and human cognition" (Finn, 2017, loc. 160), so the multidisciplinary terrain is vast indeed. Since the series is based on the shorter Routledge Focus format, it can be nimble and responsive to emerging areas of debate in fast-changing technological domains and their sociocultural impacts.

References

Amoore, L. (2020). *Cloud ethics: Algorithms and the attributes of ourselves and others.* Duke University Press.

Andrejevic, M. (2020). *Automated media.* Taylor and Francis.

Bucher, T. (2018). *If . . . Then: Algorithmic power and politics.* Oxford University Press.

Finn, E. (2017). *What algorithms want: Imagination in the age of computing.* MIT Press. Kindle version.

Hong, S. H. (2020). *Technologies of speculation: The limits of knowledge in a data-driven society.* New York University Press.

Noble, S. U. (2018). *Algorithms of oppression.* New York University Press. Kindle version.

O'Neil, C. (2016). *Weapons of math destruction.* Broadway Books. Kindle version.

Pasquale, F. (2015). *The black box society.* Harvard University Press. Kindle version.

Volume Introduction

The internet in general and social media in particular have relativized, through their global, complex and instantaneous information flows, assumptions about truth and authority in fact-based content. This has created new opportunities for state actors to use information beyond traditional conceptions of propaganda to directly assault a public's conception of reality. Additionally, almost anyone has the capability to challenge evidential claims through narratives and imagery alone as there is a wide appetite online for alternative realities. This requires new approaches to media literacy in education, the creative arts and our acts of media consumption and dissemination.

Chapter 1—"#dominant Voices in the New *Disinformation Order*" by Sara Monaci—discusses how disinformation has been used to affect public opinion. The recent pandemic crisis has seen government leaders and everyday people taking on the role of social media influencers and propagating disinformation and conspiracy theories. The chapter finds empirical evidence from a Twitter case study in the Italian context that opinion leaders and dominating voices disseminate online deception. In the spread of disinformation, leaders' social networks operate as catalysts and amplifiers. This suggests a strategy to redirect the audience from a prominent platform to "below the radar" channels with more radical ideas.

Chapter 2—"Curse or Cure? The Role of Algorithm in Promoting or Countering Information Disorder" by Taeyoung Lee and Chenyan Jia—analyzes how online deception, misinformation and mal-information have caused information disorder. While these are not necessarily novel phenomena, the digitally connected world has offered unparalleled challenges in the scale and complexity of mitigating the social impacts. Algorithms are ambivalent as they can originate, distribute and amplify information disorder, but they can also identify and aid content moderation. While new algorithmic techniques are needed to address the problem, so also are new ways to help people become less susceptible to disinformation in their media sources.

Chapter 3—"For the Sake of Sharing: Fake News as Memes" by Raúl Rodríguez-Ferrándiz, Cande Sánchez-Olmos and Tatiana Hidalgo-Marí—examines how much fake news mimics memes in its appearance and appeal. The lighthearted and consensual qualities of memes are compatible with fake news' partisan, ideologically skewed and misleading qualities. Fake news, like memes, goes viral; mutates; and adapts to different situations. Fakes news adopts and adapts the communication strategies of memes to ensure its wider dissemination.

Chapter 4—"AIBO—An Emotionally Intelligent Artificial Intelligence Brainwave Opera—Or I Built a "Sicko" AI, and So Can You" by Ellen Pearlman—presents a new media artwork, Artificial Intelligent Brainwave Opera (AIBO), which used GPT-2 to generate a "sicko" AI model. AIBO was a cloud-based character that interacted with a human performer wearing a brain computer interface. To create the "sicko AI," 47 copyright-free works about monsters, human dysfunction, power and dominance from the late 1800s through the 1940s were used to seed the character. The work shows how easy it is to create a nonhuman AI that expresses unethical norms.

Michael Filimowicz

Acknowledgment

The chapter summaries here have in places drawn from the authors' chapter abstracts, the full versions of which can be found in Routledge's online reference for the volume.

1 #dominant Voices in the New *Disinformation Order*

Sara Monaci

Information Disorder and Disinformation

In order to describe the state of the art of information disorder, recurring concepts in the literature refer to *disinformation, post-truth* and fake news. As it is well known, the term "post-truth"—word of the year in 2016 according to the *Oxford Dictionary*—describes "circumstances in which objective facts are less influential in shaping public opinion than appeals to emotions and personal beliefs" (Del Vicario et al., 2018). The term can be linked to the concept of fake news insofar as post-truths are based on objectively false news; in reality, post-truths could refer to only partially fake news that is combined with unsubstantiated facts. What is certain is that the realm of information disorder eludes precise definition or dichotomous distinction between what is true and what is false but includes nuanced forms of objective news, disseminated together with unverified or verifiable data, news that is only verisimilar or what is commonly referred to as conspiracy theories. The extremely fragmented picture finds at least a provisional composition in the concept of *disinformation*. Among the most agreed definitions of disinformation are Bennet and Livingston's (2018):

> [I]ntentional falsehoods spread as news stories or simulated documentary formats to advance political goals. We also suggest caution in adopting the term "fake news" that has become a popular media reference on grounds that it tends to frame the problem as isolated incidents of falsehood and confusion. By contrast, disinformation invites looking at more systematic disruptions of authoritative information flows due to strategic deceptions that may appear very credible to those consuming them.
>
> (p. 124)

According to Humprecht (2019, p. 1975), the economic aspect of disinformation is also not to be underestimated when describing intentionally created false information, published on multiple websites and disseminated through social media either for profit or to exert social influence. Examples are the various forms of news-hijacking or news manipulation aimed at catching

DOI: 10.4324/9781003299936-1

attention and increasing visibility on particular websites or social pages through the well-known practice of *clickbait*. According to Iosifidis and Nicoli (2021, p. 43), in the information overabundance that characterizes online communication, a plethora of content emerges that is used either as an economic opportunity or for political and ideological purposes. According to the authors, examples of disinformation include news aimed at manipulating voters' opinions or those that, for example, conceal the pro-vax positions of parents who intend to vaccinate their children (Ecker, 2017).

In general, the authors describe the phenomenon of disinformation as the "catalyst for a *post-truth era*": a phase of political and intellectual conflict in which democratic institutions and orthodoxies are shaken to their foundations by a wave of aggressive populism (d'Ancona, 2017, p. 7). It is not the intention here to argue specifically about the concept of populism—this is beyond the scope of this chapter—but it is useful to point out how some of the characteristics of populism—that is, the systematic opposition to institutions seen as elites, the appeal to emotional content and language, the central role of a dominant leader in communicative processes—can easily reverberate in online and social media interactions. Moreover, populism tends to frame the various tensions that run through contemporary society: tensions related to changes in the institutional political setup (elections, conflicts and so on) but also—as the recent pandemic highlighted—reactions of opposition and conflict with respect to health policies, vaccination campaigns or more generally the positions of academics and physicians no longer perceived as authoritative sources of expert knowledge.

Turning Points in the Current Information Disorder

The 2016 US election campaign with Donald Trump's victory, the outcome of the Brexit referendum and the 2018 Cambridge Analytica scandal with Facebook's involvement in manipulating the personal data of millions of citizens marked a significant turning point in the field of studies on the relationship between disinformation and social media.

Increasingly, social platforms such as Facebook, YouTube, Google and Twitter have proved to be ideal spheres for disinformation campaigns aimed at favoring a political candidate or even at fomenting hate speech toward ethnic minorities, linguistic and religious minorities by parties of the populist right (Iosifidis & Nicoli, 2020, p. 29). Some have identified a programmatic and emerging "disinformation order" as the combined actions of radical right-wing parties and movements in the United States and Europe, with Russian meddling strategies in Western politics: such actions tend to destabilize public opinion, pollute political debate with fake news and conspiracy theories of various kinds, and increasingly discredit the political institutions of Western democracies (Bennett & Livingston, 2018, pp. 132–134).

The recent COVID-19 health emergency has further aggravated the state of global disinformation (Mian & Khan, 2020). The pandemic has accelerated the pervasiveness of social media as an ideal environment to obviate the need for relationships in times of forced distancing: as Deborah Lupton notes, digital media have played a very important role in COVID-19 compared to the 1990s and the HIV/AIDS emergency; however, they have facilitated the huge spread of fake news often characterized by conspiracy-type narratives.[1] The World Health Organization (WHO) has called the recent crisis not just a pandemic but precisely an infodemic, a pandemic of false information or without any scientific evidence.

Several researches have investigated, through the computational analysis of the contents of the main social platforms, the propagation of misinformation as the health emergency evolves, identifying multiple forms of misinformation. The research realized by Islam et al. (2020), for example, found three types of misinformation circulating on Facebook, Twitter, online newspapers, including the websites of fact-checking agencies, and which can have serious impacts on public health: they are identified as rumors or gossip, content stigmatizing individuals or institutions, and conspiracy theories. Examples of this are the alleged links between COVID-19 and 5G technologies, or the effects of pseudo-cures also publicized by prominent public figures: this is the case of the supposed benefits of chloroquine and hydroxychloroquine mentioned by Elon Musk and Donald Trump among others (Liu et al., 2020) or the exploitation of green pass as a mean of mass digital surveillance endorsed by the European Commission[2] or the role of the so-called Big Pharma in the mass vaccination campaigns across Europe, which have been among the recurrent online misinformation narratives (Monaci & Persico, 2022). The infodemic phenomenon during the COVID-19 pandemic had important consequences for public health (Rocha et al., 2021) by increasing manifestations of depression and social anxiety also linked to a climate of suspicion and fear toward those individuals perceived as possible carriers of the virus.

Other authors have underlined with great alarm the increase in disinformation not only on the virus but also on the social perception of vaccines, emphasizing how precisely the widespread suspicion on the vaccination campaigns undertaken by the various governments urgently calls for the need for medical-scientific institutions to adopt new strategies for health communication on the web, aimed at raising awareness on the usefulness and effectiveness of vaccines, and not only those for COVID-19 (Dib et al., 2022). Several studies also found that disinformation, in its various forms, had both

---

1 D. Lupton, *Social Research for a COVID and Post-COVID World: An Initial Agenda*, March 29, 2020, https://medium.com/@deborahalupton/social-research-for-a-covid-and-post-covid-world-an-initial-agenda-796868f1fb0e

2 www.byoblu.com/2022/01/24/green-pass-sorveglianza-e-controllo-progetto-unione-europea/; Byoblu is a popular misinformation source reported by fact-checkers' black lists such as www.butac.it/the-black-list/ and Open, www.open.online/author/david-puente/

mainstream media (Soares & Recuero, 2021) and the online headlines of mainstream newspapers as its preferred sources. The data reveals that official sources contribute as much as independent sites to online infodemia. The research by Cinelli et al. (2020), for example, carried out an analysis of various social media such as Twitter, Instagram, YouTube, Reddit and Gab studying the dissemination of content related to COVID-19 and found, following the information epidemic model, that the volume of misinformation produced by trustworthy sources did not differ much from that produced by alternative, unreliable sources (profiles of private citizens, unaccredited associations or organizations, sources recognized as unreliable and so on).

Other studies show that conspiracy theories are among the most widespread fake news in times of pandemic (Leòn et al., 2022), often from sources considered reliable such as mainstream media (Papakyriakopoulos et al., 2020). Between January and March 2020, the researchers identified 11,023 unique URLs—where the URLs represent the online sources of the information—that relate to the causes of COVID-19 and appear in 267,084 posts between Facebook, Twitter, Reddit and 4chan. The researchers found that among these URLs, alternative sources had generated more information aimed at reinforcing conspiracy theories than traditional sources. However, "conspiracy" stories from traditional sources reached many more users. Furthermore, the researchers further quantified the dynamics of conspiracy theories in the social ecosystem, finding that stories that reinforced conspiracy theories generally had a higher virality than neutral stories or those aimed at debunking.

The Role of Social Media in Disinformation

In an attempt to identify the causes or enablers of disinformation, many studies focused on the role of social media. With particular reference to the period 2015–2018, a period that coincides with both the election of Donald Trump and the subsequent Cambridge Analytica scandal, many studies have noted how the strategic use of social media—Twitter and Facebook in particular—geared toward propaganda, the dissemination of fake news and the discrediting of the mainstream media, has allowed organizations and actors of the populist right to gain high visibility (Benkler et al., 2018; Splendore, 2018).

Alongside the strategic and instrumental use of social media as platforms for disinformation, many have also highlighted the role of refined artificial intelligence-based technologies in spreading what Howard called "computational propaganda" (Woolley & Howard, 2018). This can take the form of bots or trolls; they can be coordinated by troll armies, which has been outlined in Facebook's regular. As its head of security policy states, Facebook defines this (in clear terms) as together to mislead others about who they are or what they are doing". Occasionally datasets become available (from Twitter or other researchers) that purport to be collections of tweets from these inauthentic, coordinated activists, after which scholars (among other efforts) try to make sense of what signals can be used to detect them (Roeder, 2018).

Another, more recent example is artificial intelligence (AI) systems based on neural networks—such as the GPT-2–4 system[3] (Martino et al., 2020) capable of creating fake social profiles that interact in a natural way with other profiles by simulating political opinions and then taking part in a discussion in such a way as to make such systems essentially indistinguishable from real profiles.

More recently—also in connection with the new American elections in 2020 and following the assault on Capitol Hill—a new dimension of social disinformation has emerged in the public debate and academic literature: the strategic role of *fringe* or *below-the-radar platforms* (Rogers, 2021; Boccia Artieri et al., 2021). These include environments such as 4chan, Gab, 8Kun and Reddit: these guarantee high levels of anonymity and make free speech an absolute value. They have often been described as environments for the expression of subcultures or marginal cultures if not directly as cultural terrains for hate speech and expressions of misogynistic, xenophobic character and the dissemination of conspiracy theories of various inspiration (Nagle, 2017). On the occasion of the assault on Capitol Hill, circles such as 4Chan and Gab were pointed out as environments where the massive dissemination of misinformation and the sharing of fake news were important factors in strengthening the group identity of the assailants and were decisive factors in leading the group of extremist assailants to the action of January 6, 2021 (Rudden, 2021).

In general, platforms such as Reddit and 4chan offer low-quality news (junk news or pink slime news) often generated by automated profiles aimed at spreading junk content or even algorithmically generated. The study by Burton and Koehorst (2020), through a comparative analysis of the Reddit and 4chan platforms on American political news, highlights some important features: on the one hand, it emphasizes that "[m]ainstream news sources make up much of the political information that circulates on 4chan and Reddit and neither platform seem susceptible to 'pink slime'" (ibid. p. 3), and that instead it appears that a good deal of the low-quality content is linked to the two platforms via links to YouTube and the content of what the authors call the alternative influencer network (AIN): a network of influencers who are very active on YouTube—such as Joe Rogan and his channel Powerful JRE or Ben Shapiro and the Daily Wire channel—and who often take controversial or

---

3   https://en.wikipedia.org/wiki/GPT-2

decidedly provocative positions with regard to the facts of American politics. It is difficult to argue that influencers are objectively sources of disinformation: their positions can often be decidedly conservative or provocative, but this does not mean that they can be categorized as sources of disinformation.

Similarly, the study by Rogers (2021), who analyzed with a computational approach the engagement on different political content on Facebook, Twitter, Instagram, TikTok, 4chan, Reddit and Google Web Search, shows that the role of the different platforms is decidedly more oriented to "marginalize" the news content conveyed by the mainstream media. The analysis identified several strategies in this sense: TikTok for example tends to parody the news, while Instagram offers an "honest" picture mediated by its influencers who rarely deal with politics; on Facebook there is a relative decrease in content related to daily political events, while Twitter is the only platform where a hyper-partisan attitude toward political content emerges. Undoubtedly, as the author concludes, the platforms' editorial policies in recent years have contributed a great deal to curbing the dissemination of unverified information and the dissemination of content detrimental to individual and collective dignity (hate speech, xenophobia and so on): content removal and user flagging of offensive or false content, or even demonetization initiatives referring to influential profiles, have enabled platforms to significantly "clean up" information clutter and eliminate—in the worst cases—sources of information that are toxic or harmful to public debate.

Analyzing the dynamics of disinformation in a hybrid media ecosystem is a complex challenge: as we have seen, limits to the undertaking emerge both from analyses that focus on social media and disinformation-enabling technologies and from investigations that identify subcultural platforms as privileged breeding grounds for disinformation. Generally speaking, the relationship between social media and legacy media (TV and the like) is most often controversial and characterized by relations influenced by opportunistic priorities—for example, exploiting the popularity of certain questionable sources on social media to capture the audience attention—or on the other hand, relations determined by a clear opposition with respect to the online information flow.

A further dimension that must be taken into account is that of the active players—the influencers or opinion leaders—in disinformation. During the recent health emergency we have seen on the media level the growing role of medical-scientific authorities in the public debate: this phenomenon is unprecedented since the expert knowledge is normally quite detached from the show-business logic of the mass media. Science work is perceived more as background work, albeit with great influence on the political decision-maker. On the other hand, the political opinion leaders understood in the traditional sense have had great relevance: some of them immediately seized the opportunity of the health emergency to further strengthen their leadership, bypassing, as in Italy for example, the normal parliamentary procedures in adopting emergency measures; others like Trump and Bolsonaro have tried to minimize the effects of the pandemic; other leaders have seized the opportunity to politically manipulate the debate on vaccines and the certifications adopted (e.g., the green pass) in a perspective of defending fundamental individual freedoms. In general, the public debate linked to the recent pandemic has certainly been marked by an increase in disinformation—both in the legacy media and in social media—where the role of opinion leaders has been relevant in increasing the general information disorder.

The chapter focuses on the role of disinformation during the recent health crisis; the scope of observation allows for an analysis of the complementary interaction between some of the different factors analyzed in the previous sections: on the one hand, the role of opinion leaders in the dissemination of disinformation, and on the other hand, the bias of relevant social platforms in the public debate—in particular Twitter—together with the productive and diffusive role of below-the-radar platforms.

The recent pandemic and its misinformation have had both global and local repercussions: it is worth considering, for example, impacts on vaccination campaigns undertaken all over the world and the difficulties in countering the spread of conspiracy theories related to vaccines or their alleged long-term effects. Social media played a central role in the information ecosystem of the pandemic, as did their instrumental use by opinion leaders who deliberately helped to fuel rather than defuse the growing polarization of public opinion.

The Role of Opinion Leaders in Misinformation About COVID-19

Multiple researches highlight the important role of political opinion leaders, who in both social and legacy media often contribute to information disorder. This is the case, for example, with many populist governments such as Bolsonaro's government in Brazil (Soares et al., 2021)—one of the countries hardest hit by COVID-19—where the risks associated with the spread of the virus have long been downplayed, as have the government's initiatives to contain the pandemic. Even in the United States, former President Donald Trump in 2020 considered the damage of the pandemic to be minimal and recommended home remedies to treat COVID-19 infection (Rabin & Cameron, 2020; Facher, 2020).

Italy is a relevant case study as a nation with significant populist forces, which often rely on disinformation. In particular, the recent online debate has been characterized by harsh criticism of the role of political institutions—at a national and European level—in the health emergency: conspiracy theories such as the alleged relationship between 5G technologies and the spread of COVID-19, or the exploitation of the green pass as a means of mass digital surveillance promoted by the European Commission, or the role of the so-called Big Pharma complex in mass vaccination campaigns across Europe, have been among the most prominent disinformation narratives online. Disinformation content has heavily characterized the national media ecosystem, often colonized by populist political actors seeking visibility and opportunities to amplify their party agendas. The strategic use of disinformation as a means to increase online reputation and popularity and their impact on national and European institutions has become particularly evident, for example, in the positions taken by political actors such as Claudio Borghi and Francesca Donato at different levels, both through social media and their institutional activities in the Italian and European parliaments.

Among the most controversial topics in the recent Italian debate, that on the green pass[4] has emerged particularly clearly. The debate has long been polarized between opinions in favor of the restrictions and libertarian positions that are decidedly critical of the government's measures, which are considered detrimental to freedom of opinion, freedom of movement and individual privacy. The debate developed both in parliamentary chambers and on Twitter, with the intervention of institutional figures such as political actors, journalists, opinion makers, but also millions of private citizens divided by hyper-partisan positions and so on. The debate was also characterized by an increase in disinformation in social media, a phenomenon that could also be partly attributable to the role of active profiles and their social networks of reference (Spitale et al., 2022; Caliandro et al., 2020). The chapter presents some evidence of the significant role in the Twitter debate of some Italian opinion leaders of a purely populist nature. Through a computational approach to data analysis, the contribution also highlights their communication and social networking strategies aimed at spreading disinformation and fake news content.

Opinion Leaders on Twitter: Keepers of Information or Multipliers of Fake News?

Studies on the relationship between the media and opinion leadership refer to the contribution of Katz and Lazarsfeld (1955) and the two-stage communication model according to which prominent figures in the public debate—*opinion leaders*—*play* a relevant role in disseminating information from the mass media to the wider public. The model emphasizes the strategic role of interpersonal communication in mediating the unidirectional relationship between broadcast media and wider audiences. Katz and Lazarsfeld identify four salient characteristics of the opinion leader: having a large following, being considered an "expert" in a specific field, being popular and assuming a central position within a network in which they can exert influence and

---

4 *Green pass* is the name of the certificate attesting to the completion of the anti-COVID-19 vaccination cycle or recovery from COVID-19; www.dgc.gov.it/web/

positive reinforcement. The model has had great impact on multiple studies and multidisciplinary perspectives, for example, in the field of marketing, political science and analyses on the diffusion of innovation (Rogers, 2003; Shah & Scheufele, 2006; Van den Bulte & Joshi, 2007).

The emergence of social platforms calls into question the relevance of Katz and Lazarsfeld's model: a first observation, put forward by Dubois and Gaffney (2014), describes how the characteristics of opinion leadership described by the model are effectively operationalized by the affordances of Twitter, thanks, for instance, to the follow/be-followed features, the multimedia dimensions of content that enhance the visibility of profiles and the immediacy of interactions (e.g., mentions, retweets, likes and so on) that establish *social networks* between popular profiles. The contemporary social media landscape also makes the role of opinion leaders as "gatekeepers" of political information questionable. Although traditional opinion leaders had privileged access to the sources of the political agenda, digital media have significantly changed the dynamics of communication flows. According to Park (2013), it is credible that Twitter opinion leaders are involved in a "multistage flow" process, rather than the traditional "two-stage flow" process: a multistage flow in fact distributes information through a myriad of intermediate channels. Twitter's "more connected" audiences play an important role here in the creation and distribution of information through multiple channels, compared to individuals with fewer connections; moreover, opinion leaders nowadays also elaborate content independently of party agendas and share it directly to their audiences. It is reasonable to assume, therefore, that in social media, a "multiphase flow" of communication involves both opinion leaders understood as traditional political actors (e.g., leaders of political parties, representatives of institutions) and individuals acting as *influencers* on a specific topic in the online debate. Opinion leaders can thus also be identified among private citizens who are influential precisely by virtue of their intense interaction with their followers and the online network of other political actors.

In the relevant literature, the role of opinion leaders in social media is referred to as a positive reinforcement of civic and political debate (Alexandre et al., 2021; Park, 2013; Vicari et al., 2020): opinion leaders can be reliable sources of information and thus protect their followers from fake news, or they can themselves be "amplifiers" of disinformation and activators of echo chambers (Dubois et al., 2020). Echo chambers can be shaped either intentionally or unintentionally. The former typically involve bots (Alexandre et al., 2021): fictitious profiles that massively retweet content and hashtags aimed at increasing the visibility of a topic or other profiles. Unintentionally formed echo chambers could result from what Cass Sunstein has described as *reputational cascades* (2018, pp. 98–101): the phenomenon whereby information, which may also include fake news or conspiracy theories, is multiplied on Twitter due to the "reputation of the source" and its being perceived—as in the case of influential profiles—as an opinion leader within a particular social network (Monaci & Persico, 2022).

Several studies tend to downplay the impact of echo chambers on individual opinions (Dubois & Blank, 2018; Flaxman et al., 2016; Fletcher & Park, 2017); nevertheless, if these are focused on particularly verbose, popular or influential profiles, the overall effect can be amplified. In the context of the impeachment trial of former Brazilian president Dilma Rousseff for example, the phenomenon of Twitter echo chambers was particularly evident: the role of opinion leaders stood out precisely because of massive retweeting activity (Alexandre et al., 2021, p. 4) highlighting how Twitter networks can reinforce "partisan positions" through active sharing of information within user groups.

Analysis Methodologies

Data Collection

The data collected on Twitter refers to a six-month period: from June 15 to December 14, 2021.5 The period corresponds to the measures taken by the Italian Prime Minister Mario Draghi in relation to the green pass; 4,307,487 tweets were collected from 217,978 unique users. The tweets are in Italian and contain the keywords "green pass" or "supergreen pass." In the six-month period observed, a number of "discussion peaks" were identified relating to legislative activities (e.g., Decree Law 23 July 2021), that is, significant events: the no-green pass demonstration in Trieste in October 2021 or the multiple no-vax street demonstrations in autumn 2021. The following are the identified discussion peaks (Figure 1.1):

- July 12–16, 2021: debate on the announced decree law on green pass constraints.
- July 20–30, 2021: on July 23, Mario Draghi issues a decree law on the mandating of green passes for access to recreational activities, restaurants, bars, cinemas, sports areas and international mobility.
- August 4–13, 2021: the decree-law comes into force on August 6.
- September 14–21, 2021: schools reopen and the debate over green pass constraints increases.
- October 08–20, 2021: on October 15, the green pass becomes compulsory for access to workplaces; as a result street protests are animated especially in northern Italy.[6]
- November 22–26, 2021: the debate grows on the super green pass mandate.

---

5 Data collection was carried out with TCAT (Twitter Capture and Analysis Toolset), 4CAT; https://wiki.digitalmethods.net/Dmi/ToolDmiTcat
   The dataset is available at https://doi.org/10.5281/zenodo.6424693
6 www.open.online/2021/10/21/trieste-manifestazione-venerdi-22-ottobre-allarme-infiltrati-violenti/

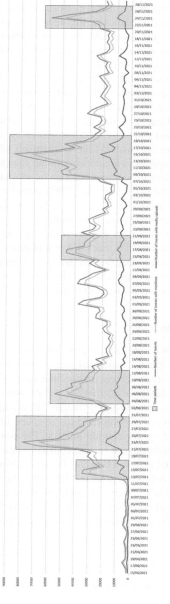

Figure 1.1 Discussion peaks between June 15 and December 14, 2021

#dominant Voices and Social Network Analysis

To identify opinion leaders on Twitter, the critical metrics described by Rogers (2018) were used and in particular the *dominant voices*—"the specific actors that give voice to the issue with the greatest strength"; also "which sources are given in an (authoritative) issue space, and of those, which dominate and which speaking subjects are cut down or marginalized" (ibid., p. 468). The metric was operationalized through the number of mentions in the tweet dataset and the most mentioned profiles were considered the dominant voices in the considered debate. Using this metric, we then identified the most retweeted profiles, those that had the most interactions (e.g., tweets in response to their posts) and those most mentioned by other profiles. Consistent with other studies on Twitter (Cha & Gummadi, 2010; Sousa, 2010), we thus measured interactions in the network rather than mere visibility. The dominant voices also allow us to measure a significant characteristic of influence as described by Katz and Lazarsfeld (1955), namely: "being considered as an expert, being knowledgeable." Next, we applied social network analysis (SNA) to identify connections between the dominant voices in the debate. We applied SNA to several subsets of data corresponding to Twitter discussion peaks using GEPHI software.[7] For each discussion peak, a network analysis of mentions was performed, focusing on the users who interacted with the most other Twitter profiles to highlight the recipients of their mentions and the relationships between the different opinion leaders.

Where Is the Disinformation?

Two different approaches were used to examine whether and to what extent the identified opinion leaders facilitated the dissemination of disinformation such as conspiracy-type content and/or fake news. Firstly, a qualitative analysis of the opinion leaders in the Twitter debate was conducted to define their position with respect to green pass policies.[8] In the second step, we used TCAT to analyze the types of sources (e.g., YouTube links or videos from other platforms) shared by the opinion leaders. The analysis of the shared sources is significant with respect to two considerations: the first concerns the usefulness of external links in obviating Twitter's 280-character limit; this makes it possible to offer broader arguments than concise tweets and in some cases, as already noted in the literature, to argue more convincingly against anti-COVID-19 vaccinations (Chen & Milojevic, 2018). This evidence leads to the hypothesis that the links shared by green pass opponents could lead to

---

7 https://gephi.org/
8 The qualitative analysis was based on the desktop analysis of the most frequently mentioned Twitter profiles.

questionable content and sources on the topic. Next, we applied SNA to analyze whether interactions between opinion leaders and questionable sources
had fueled the spread of misinformation. The analysis focused on the discussion peaks is described in Figure 1.1.

The Results of the Data Analysis

The Dominant Voices of Opinion Leaders

The analysis of *mentions* revealed a very limited number of dominant voices:
by selecting the profiles with more than 30,000 mentions in the defined
period (June—December 2021), a list of 18 opinion leaders was defined (Figures 1.2). Figure 1.3 also shows the interactions between the most frequently
mentioned opinion leaders during the six-month observation period.

The dominant role of the @borghi_claudio profile is evident with more than
170,000 mentions. It is followed by a list of profiles with far fewer mentions.
Claudio Borghi represents an opinion leader in the traditional sense: he is a member of the Italian parliament and belongs to the Lega Nord party. His relevance
as an accredited expert on the green pass issue is particularly evident on Twitter,
where he stands out as the most retweeted and quoted profile. His profile also
counts the highest number of interactions such as comments, replies; moreover,
by virtue of his relationship with parliament, his position allows him to mediate
the Lega Nord's anti-green pass positions to the wider online audience.

Together with Claudio Borghi, the most mentioned profiles are private
citizens—@valy_s, @FmMosca, @ortigia_p, @fdragoni, @giuliomarini2—
or other political actors: @ladyonorato is the Twitter profile of Francesca
Donato, MEP; @matteosalvinimi belongs to Matteo Salvini, leader of the

@Username	@mentions received
borghi_claudio	174,864
Valy_s	72,353
FmMosca	69,079
fdragoni	68,913
dottorbarbieri	47,051
LaVeritaWeb	44,207
ladyonorato	43,856
byoblu	41,428
Lorenzo62752880	41,417
OrtigiaP	40,542
GiulioMarini2	37,484
AzzurraBarbuto	34,287
Intuslegens	34,112

Figure 1.2 The most frequently mentioned profiles
in the overall dataset

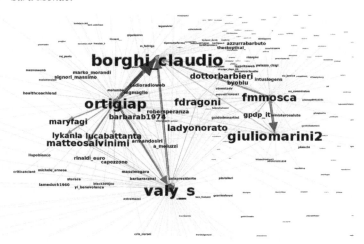

Figure 1.3 The analysis of the mention network including opinion leaders in the six-
month observation period

Northern League; @byoblu is a popular Italian source of disinformation and
conspiracy theories,[9] with over 41,000 mentions. We found only @repubblica
(the national daily newspaper *La Repubblica*) among the mainstream media
profiles with 30,600 mentions. The qualitative analysis of the content tweeted
by the dominant profiles (except @repubblica) highlights their critical stance
toward the adoption of the green pass and the restrictions imposed by the
government.

Opinion Leader Networks

In order to analyze the possible interactions between the opinion leader profiles, we performed an analysis of the mentions made or received by the users.
Initially, using TCAT, we selected the "social graph by mentions" feature
including all users to generate the six. GDF files to be processed with GEPHI;
we then modeled the graph with GEPHI, performing the same steps for each
time period. We found a continuous and prevalent presence of @claudio_
borghi along with a limited number of other profiles that tweeted with particular intensity, as shown by the significant size of their nodes in Figures 1.4, 1.5,

9 ByoBlu is on several "blacklists" of fact-checking agencies such as BUTAC; www.butac.it/
   tag/the-black-list/, or Open www.open.online/2020/08/07/mini-bomba-atomica-nel-porto-di-
   beirut-tre-fisici-rispondono-ad-alessandro-meluzzi-chef-rubio-e-byoblu/

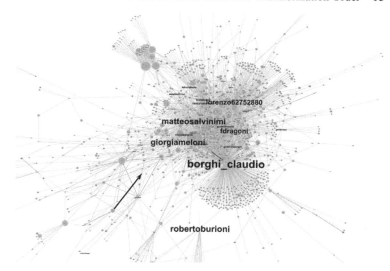

Figure 1.4 The mention network in period A: July 12–16, 2021

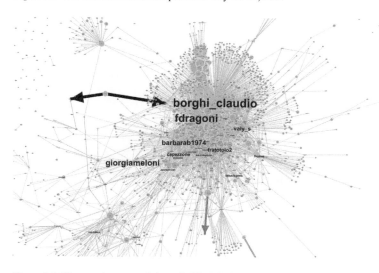

Figure 1.5 The mention network in period B: July 20–30, 2021

1.6, 1.7, 1.8 and 1.9. The latter include the profiles of private citizens opposed to the green pass already mentioned in the general graph (e.g., @valy_s, @FmMosca, @ortigia_p and so on), along with other profiles, such as

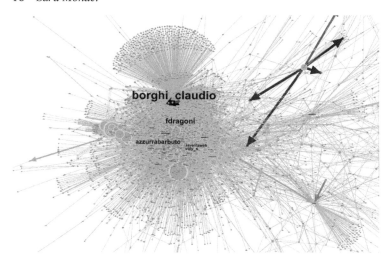

Figure 1.6 The mention network in period C: August 4–13, 2021

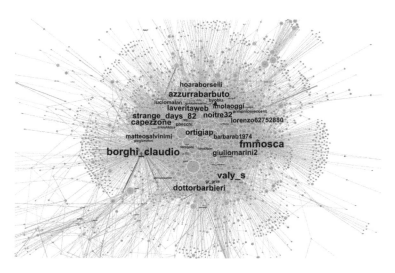

Figure 1.7 The mention network in period D: September 14–21, 2021

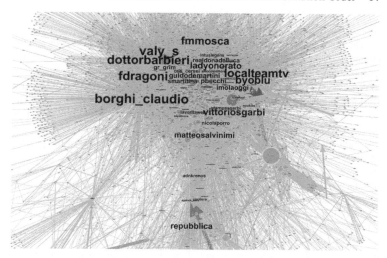

Figure 1.8 The mention network in period E: October 8–20, 2021

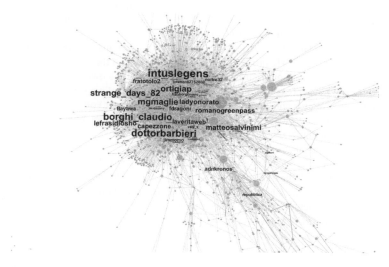

Figure 1.9 The mention network in period F: November 22–26, 2021

prominent political actors (@giorgiameloni, @capezzone and so on), and sources of disinformation such as @byoblu and @imolaoggi.[10]

The analysis of the network of mentions in the discussion peaks reveals the evolution of the debate and the positions of the opinion leaders: the progressive marginalization of the pro-green pass voices compared to the opposing opinions is evident. Period A (Figure 1.4) reflects the significant presence of Roberto Burioni[11] on the network, which however tends to disappear in later periods. The same process affects mainstream media profiles, such as @repubblica and @ corriere, which were barely visible in the first period. In period B (Figure 1.5), @borghi_claudio maintains a central position, and the relevance of the profiles of other political actors increases, such as @giorgiameloni and @capezzone (the former belonging to Giorgia Meloni, leader of the right-wing party Fratelli d'Italia, and the latter to Daniele Capezzone, a member of Forza Italia). Both opinion leaders represent a firm opposition, both online and in their parliamentary activities, to the Draghi decree approving the mandatory green pass. In periods D and E (Figures 1.7 and 1.8), it is interesting to note the increasing visibility of @byoblu's disinformation profile. In the E period, other information profiles openly opposed to the green pass, and often sources of fake news and conspiracy theories are added, such as @imolaoggi. In the last period F (Figure 1.9) another highly questionable profile emerges in close connection with the main network—@mgmaglie—whose role is explored in the next section.

The in-depth analysis of the relationships in social networks describes the dissemination processes of the opinion leaders' content. Claudio Borghi is definitely the one most mentioned by the other users, although he hardly mentions the other opinion leaders (Figure 1.10).

@borghi_claudio is particularly busy tweeting original content or even retweeting himself. He produced almost 1,000 tweets in the period analyzed, of which 50% were original tweets, 20% retweets of his own tweets and the remaining 30% retweets of other profiles. In total, 70% of his voice is focused on multiplying his anti-green pass position. The dominant voices in his social network (private citizens rather than political actors) interacted massively with him and a few others (Figure 1.11).

It is possible that these profiles used Claudio Borghi's visibility to increase their own popularity, using a hashtag-hijacking strategy (Mousavi & Ouyang, 2021): in general, the interactions in Claudio Borghi's social network reveal an extremely segregated debate that is articulated in a small number of profiles that mostly only interact with each other and are united by a critical stance toward the green pass. The network of users can be regarded as an echo chamber due to the verbose tweeting activity of opinion leaders; it is also noteworthy that the leaders' retweets often spread disinformation and conspiracy theories, such as

---

10 According to the fact-checking site Bufale.net, the Imolaoggi site has a clear role in spreading false, xenophobic and Islamophobic information; see www.bufale.net/guida-utile-chi-ce-dietro-il-sito-imolaoggi-bufale-net/

11 Roberto Burioni is an Italian virologist, physician and academic among the most authoritative voices in favor of the mass vaccination campaign against COVID-19 in Italy;

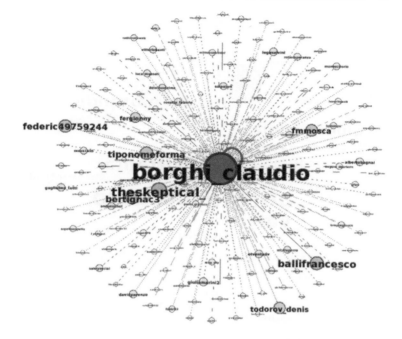

Figure 1.10 The green nodes are the main profiles retweeted by Claudio Borghi

the YouTube videos on Maria Giovanna Maglie retweeted by Borghi and those spread by other opinion leaders through the video platform Rumble.

How Disinformation Spreads

In order to trace the links between the role of opinion leaders in spreading disinformation, both direct relationships between a profile and disinformation sources and relationships mediated by other profiles were analyzed. In the first case, we analyzed the links to YouTube or other web pages identified in the content tweeted by opinion leaders. Claudio Borghi, for instance, tweeted at least 40 hyperlinks to videos from two YouTube channels, Inriverente[12] and L'Anticonformista.[13] Both channels act as a sounding board for the parliamentarian, reinforcing the visibility of his positions on the world's best-known video platform. However, the two channels feature other actors, such as Maria Giovanna Maglie,[14] spokesperson for even more radical positions.

12 www.youtube.com/results?search_query=Inriverente
13 www.youtube.com/c/Lanticonformista
14 Maria Giovanna Maglie is a well-known Italian journalist and columnist; https://it.wikipedia.org/wiki/Maria_Giovanna_Maglie

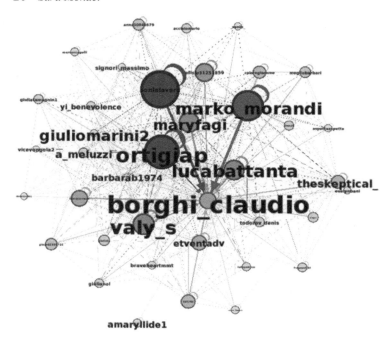

Figure 1.11 The purple nodes are the main profiles retweeted by Claudio Borghi

The channel L'Anticonformista shows a video in which Borghi introduces the book written by Maglie, *Damned Italians*, where the author reiterates the need "to fight Taliban-vaccinist television, resist the health dictatorship" and to call for "mass screening campaigns before vaccination to assess the potentially harmful effects of vaccines."[15] The same arguments can be found in a four-hour video live on the Inriverente channel, where Maglie talks to the online audience about vaccines, the green pass, and the like, repeatedly invoking the "resistance" of the "no-vax people."[16] Borghi's tweets, with links to the two YouTube channels, were retweeted 2,461 times during the period analyzed.

Among the other direct sources, at least 5,000 links to videos retweeted by the video platform Rumble[17] were identified. Among the most tweeted videos

---

15 www.youtube.com/watch?v=uyflQObl36E&t=1822s
16 https://youtu.be/AlzHjD1ilCk
17 The video-sharing platform (https://rumble.com/) has repeatedly been accused of feeding disinformation and conspiracy theories such as QAnon. www.wired.com/story/rumble-

Figure 1.12 The network of profile mentions in relation to Rumble videos

is "green pass = home expropriation![18] 'which supports the thesis of being used as a tool for mass surveillance. The video states that "digital identity will be exploited by the European Community to expropriate citizens' private property. This will happen if 95 per cent of the population receives the green pass or the unique digital code."

In relation to this content, numerous opinion leader profiles were found that had already been identified in previous analyses, for example, @giulio marini2, @fmMosca, @ladyonorato and so on (Figure 1.12).

Another direct link between Borghi and sources of disinformation is @byoblu's tweet with the interview given to the web TV ByoBlu by Borghi and the anesthetist Barbara Balanzoni (whose Twitter profile is @Barbara-BalanzoniRESISTENCE) on July 26, 2021, shortly after Draghi's decree on the green pass. In this case @byoblu quotes Borghi and not the other way around: the tweet with the link to the interview was retweeted more than 1,000 times in four days, from July 24 to July 29, 2021. Balanzoni accuses fellow

---

sends-viewers-tumbling-toward-misinformation/; https://globalnews.ca/news/8451636/donald-trump-social-media-canada-rumble/
18 https://rumble.com/vps48n-green-pass-espropriazione-casa.html?mref=23gga&mrefc=7

doctors in the mainstream media of "Nazi-communism" because of their efforts to promote mass vaccination. Claudio Borghi's arguments are even more radical: regarding the possibility of extending vaccination to minors, he accuses "the Left—a certain Left—of having always had an obsession with children"—highlighting "the greed with which our children are observed by the Left." Alluding to the events in Bibbiano in 2019[19] and perhaps echoing the popular American Pizzagate of 2016[20] Borghi exploits popular conspiracy theories to reinforce his misinformation.

To examine indirect relationships, we analyzed the points of contact between Claudio Borghi's profile and Byoblu's profile mediated by other dominant profiles in the identified time periods. GEPHI made it possible to identify social networks around both Claudio Borghi and Byoblu. The intersection between these networks is highlighted in different colors (Borghi in red, Byoblu in yellow and the intersection between the two in orange), sizing nodes by rank and labels by number of mentions received. We then analyzed the overlap between the two networks over the periods studied to identify to what extent and how the intersection between the two networks favored the expansion of one of the two networks and thus the spread of disinformation. The following graphs show three different time periods: period A (Figure 1.13), period B (Figure 1.14) and period E (Figure 1.15). The first period provides a framework for the following two periods, which show a significant overlap between the Borghi and Byoblu networks.

As described earlier, on July 26 (period B), Byoblu published an interview with Borghi and promoted his visibility on its channels. The analysis shows that Borghi's ego-network remains almost stable compared to Period A; the number of nodes doubles, but the period analyzed is twice as long. At the same time, Byoblu grows significantly (almost three times) and the intersection also increases 4.75 times (from 28 to 133; normalized values) (Figure 1.16). In other words, the number of profiles mentioning Byoblu in relation to Borghi in that period increases significantly, thus expanding both the visibility of the disinformation profile and the dissemination of its content. In period E (October 8–20), the intersection grows again and the networks of Borghi and Byoblu "catch up." Figure 1.16 shows the benefits of the rapprochement above the Byoblu network, which again increases the number of mentions, both in relation to Borghi and independently of the leader.

---

19 www.corriere.it/cronache/19_luglio_19/caso-bibbiano-cosa-c-entra-pd-scontro-cinque-stelle-83e5332e-aa27–11e9-a88c-fde1fa123548.shtml
20 https://en.wikipedia.org/wiki/Pizzagate_conspiracy_theory

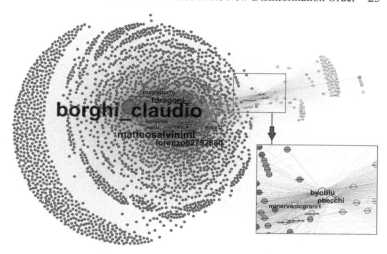

Figure 1.13 In period A, the two networks are relatively far apart, and the Byoblu network is relatively small

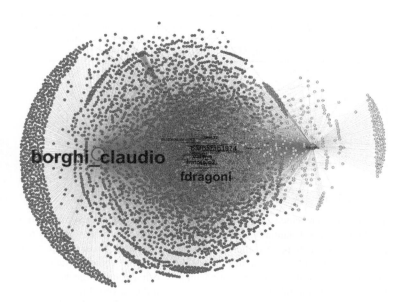

Figure 1.14 In period B the two networks increasingly overlap, and the Byoblu network grows

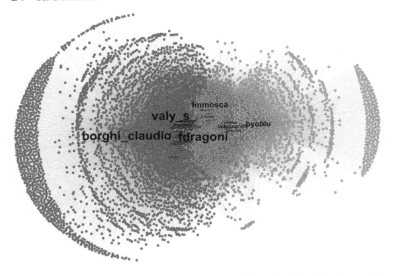

Figure 1.15 In period E the two networks overlap significantly, with a clear increase in the network around Byoblu

Period	Length (days)	Dimension		Union ∪	Intersection ∩	Normalized ∩ ∩norm
		EGO_borghi	EGO_byoblu			
A	5	2.626	247	2.729	144	28.8
B	11	5.444	1.788	5.761	1.471	133.7
C	10	5.275	1.160	5.662	773	77.3
D	8	3.365	985	3.890	460	57.5
E	13	5.285	2.659	6.499	1.445	111.2
F	5	1.884	452	2.164	172	34.4

Figure 1.16 The evolution of ego networks in the discussion peaks

Conclusions

The research presented reveals a Twitter debate strongly concentrated on a single position substantially critical of the green pass and with very few relevant voices able to oppose alternative positions. Mainstream newspapers are marginal in the observed period, as are the influential voices on television that play a central role in promoting mass vaccination and the green-pass instrument. On the other hand, the analysis identifies a very limited number of dominant voices around the figure of opinion leader Claudio Borghi who is able to mediate the no-green-pass positions shared by a large majority of his party to the connected public. The specific dimensions of opinion leadership on Twitter are identified in the dissemination of disinformation, where social networks around leaders act as important catalysts and amplifiers of fake news and conspiracy theories, such as those tweeted by Borghi through YouTube videos on Maria Giovanna Maglie and by other leaders through the video platform Rumble. This also points to a strategy aimed at diverting the public from a main platform to "below the radar" channels such as Rumble (Boccia Artieri et al., 2021) where positions tend to be more radical. The results show that disinformation sources, such as Byoblu, interact openly with opinion leaders on Twitter to increase their visibility by multiplying the overall volume of disinformation. The relationship can be direct or mediated by other profiles acting as influencers. This emphasizes the specificity of a multi-lateral communication process as one of the specific dynamics of opinion leadership on Twitter and thus a substantially different dynamic from that assumed by Katz and Lazarsfeld's model and more akin to the multivocality of social.

References

Alexandre, I., Jai-sung Yoo, J., & Murthy, D. (2021). Making tweets great again: Who are opinion leaders, and what did they tweet about Donald Trump? *Social Science Computer Review.* https://doi.org/10.1177/08944393211008859

Benkler, Y., Faris, R., & Roberts, H. (2018). *Network propaganda: Manipulation, disinformation, and radicalization in American politics.* Oxford University Press.

Bennett, W. L., & Livingston, S. (2018). The disinformation order: Disruptive communication and the decline of democratic institutions. *European Journal of Communication, 33*(2), 122–139. https://doi.org/10.1177/0267323118760317

Boccia Artieri, G., Brilli, S., & Zurovac, E. (2021). Below the radar: Private groups, locked platforms, and ephemeral content. Introduction to the special issue. *Social Media + Society, 7*(1).

Burton, A. G., & Koehorst, D. (2020). Research note: The spread of political misinformation on online subcultural platforms. *HKS Misinfo Rev, 1*(6), 10-37016.

Caliandro, A., Anselmi, G., & Sturiale, V. (2020). Fake news, Covid-19 and Infodemia: An example of real-time social research on Twitter. *Mediascapes Journal* (15), 174–188.

Cha, M., & Gummadi, K. P. (2010). Measuring user influence in Twitter: The million follower fallacy. *International AAAI Conference on Weblogs and Social Media, 10,* 10–17.

Chen, W. C., & Milojevic, S. (2018). *Interaction or segregation: Vaccination and information sharing on twitter.* Companion of the 2018 ACM Conference on Computer Supported Cooperative Work and Social Computing, pp. 301–304.

Cinelli, M., Quattrociocchi, W., Galeazzi, A., Valensise, C. M., Brugnoli, E., Schmidt, A. L. . . . Scala, A. (2020). The covid-19 social media infodemic. *Scientific Reports, 10*(1), 1–10.

d'Ancona, M. (2017). *Post-truth: The new war on truth and how to fight back.* Random House.

Del Vicario, M., Quattrociocchi, W., Scala, A., & Zollo, F. (2018). *Polarization and fake news: Early warning of potential misinformation targets*. CoRRabs/1802.01400, 2018.

Dib, F., Mayaud, P., Chauvin, P., & Launay, O. (2022). Online mis/disinformation and vaccine hesitancy in the era of COVID-19: Why we need an eHealth literacy revolution. *Human Vaccines & Immunotherapeutics, 18*(1), 1–3.

Dubois, E., & Blank, G. (2018). The echo chamber is overstated: The moderating effect of political interest and diverse media. *Information, Communication & Society, 21*(5), 729–745.

Dubois, E., & Gaffney, D. (2014). The multiple facets of influence: Identifying political influentials and opinion leaders on Twitter. *American Behavioral Scientist, 58*(10), 1260–1277.

Dubois, E., Minaeian, S., Paquet-Labelle, A., & Beaudry, S. (2020). Who to trust on social media: How opinion leaders and seekers avoid disinformation and echo chambers. *Social Media + Society, 6*(2). https://doi.org/10.1177/2056305120913993.

Ecker, U. K. (2017). Why rebuttals may not work: The psychology of misinformation. *Media Asia, 44*(2), 79–87. https://doi.org/10.1080/01296612.2017.1384145

Facher, L. (2020). Fact-checking Trump's optimistic hydroxychloroquine claims. *Statnews.com*. https://www.statnews.com/2020/04/06/trump-hydroxychloroquine-fact-check/

Flaxman, S., Goel, S., & Rao, J. M. (2016). Filter bubbles, echo chambers, and online news consumption. *Public Opinion Quarterly, 80*(S1), 298–320.

Fletcher, R., & Park, S. (2017). The impact of trust in the news media on online news consumption and participation. *Digital Journalism, 5*(10), 1281–1299. https://doi.org/10.1080/21670811.2017.1279979

Humprecht, E. (2019). Where 'fake news' flourishes: A comparison across four Western democracies. *Information, Communication & Society, 22*(13), 1973–1988. https://doi.org/10.1080/1369118X.2018.1474241

Iosifidis, P., & Nicoli, N. (2020). *Digital democracy, social media and disinformation*. Routledge. p. 29.

Katz, E., & Lazarsfeld, P. F. (1955). *Personal influence: The part played by people in the flow of mass communications*. Transaction Publishers.

León, B., Martínez-Costa, M. P., Salaverría, R., & López-Goñi, I. (2022). Health and science-related misinformation on COVID-19: A content analysis of hoaxes identified by fact-checkers in Spain. *PLoS one, 17*(4), e0265995.

Liu, M., Caputi, T. L., Dredze, M., Kesselheim, A. S., & Ayers, J. W. (2020). Internet searches for unproven COVID-19 therapies in the United States. *JAMA Internal Medicine, 180*(8), 1116–1118.

Martino, G. D. S., Cresci, S., Barrón-Cedeño, A., Yu, S., Di Pietro, R., & Nakov, P. (2020). *A survey on computational propaganda detection*. arXiv preprint arXiv:2007.08024.

Mian, A., & Khan, S. (2020). Coronavirus: The spread of misinformation. *BMC Medicine, 18*, 89. https://doi.org/10.1186/s12916-020-01556-3.

Monaci, S., & Persico, S. (2022). Mixed analysis of user activity, content and networks: Twitter's information cascades on conspiratorial pandemics. In *The covid-19 pandemic as a challenge for media and communication studies* (pp. 157–169). Routledge.

Mousavi, P., & Ouyang, J. (2021). Detecting hashtag hijacking for hashtag activism. In *Proceedings of the 1st workshop on NLP for positive impact* (pp. 82–92). Association for Computational Linguistics (ACL).

Nagle, A. (2017). *Kill all normies: Online culture wars from 4chan and Tumblr to Trump and the alt-right*. John Hunt Publishing.

Papakyriakopoulos, O., Serrano, J. C. M., & Hegelich, S. (2020). The spread of COVID-19 conspiracy theories on social media and the effect of content moderation. *The Harvard Kennedy School Misinformation Review, 1* Special issue. https://doi.org/10.37016/mr-2020-034.

Park, C. S. (2013). Does Twitter motivate involvement in politics? Tweeting, opinion leadership, and political engagement. *Computers in Human Behavior, 29*(4), 1641–1648.

Rabin, R., & Cameron, C. (2020). Trump falsely claims "99 percent" of virus cases are 'totally harmless." *The New York Times*. https://www.nytimes.com/2020/07/05/us/politics/trump-coronavirus-factcheck.html

Rocha, Y. M., de Moura, G. A., Desidério, G. A., et al. (2021). The impact of fake news on social media and its influence on health during the COVID-19 pandemic: A systematic review. *Journal of Public Health (Berl.)*. https://doi.org/10.1007/s10389-021-01658-z

Roeder, O. (2018, August 8). We gave you 3 million Russian troll tweets. Here's what you've found so far. *FiveThirtyEight*. https://fivethirtyeight.com/features/ what-you-found-in-3-million-russian-troll-tweets/.

Rogers, E. M. (2003). *Diffusion of innovations* (5th ed.). Free Press.

Rogers, R. (2018). Otherwise engaged: Social media from vanity metrics to critical analytics. *International Journal of Communication, 12*(23), 450–472.

Rogers, R. (2021). Marginalizing the mainstream: How social media privilege political information. *Frontiers in Big Data, 4.*

Rudden, M. G. (2021). Insurrection in the US Capitol: Understanding psychotic, projective and introjective group processes. *International Journal of Applied Psychoanalytic Studies, 18*(4), 372–384.

Shah, D. V., & Scheufele, D. A. (2006). Explicating opinion leadership: Nonpolitical dispositions, information consumption, and civic participation. *Political Communication, 23*(1), 1–22. https://doi.org/10.1080/10584600500476932

Soares, F. B., & Recuero, R. (2021). How the mainstream media help to spread disinformation about covid-19. *M/C Journal, 24*(1). https://doi.org/10.5204/mcj.2735

Soares, F. B., Recuero, R., Volcan, T., Fagundes, G., & Sodré, G. (2021). Research note: Bolsonaro's firehose: How Covid-19 disinformation on WhatsApp was used to fight a government political crisis in Brazil. *The Harvard Kennedy School Misinformation Review*. https://misinforeview.hks.harvard.edu/article/research-note-bolsonaros-firehose-how-covid-19-disinformation-on-whatsapp-was-used-to-fight-a-government-political-crisis-in-brazil/

Sousa, D. (2010). *Characterization of the Twitter @ replies network: Are user ties social or topical?* Proceedings of the 2nd International Workshop on Search and Mining User-Generated Contents. https://doi.org/10.1145/1871985.1871996.

Spitale, G., Biller-Andorno, N., & Germani, F. (2022). Concerns around opposition to the green pass in Italy: Social listening analysis using a mixed methods approach. *Journal of Medical Internet Research, 24*(2), e34385.

Splendore, S. (2018). Communicative activism and political impasse: the changing media system in the context of fake news and populism. *Contemporary Italian Politics, 10*(4), 407–420.

Sunstein, C. R. (2018). *#Republic*. Princeton University Press.

Van den Bulte, C., & Joshi, Y. V. (2007). New product diffusion with influentials and imitators. *Marketing Science*, *26*(3), 400–421. https://doi.org/10.1287/mksc.1060.0224

Vicari, S., Iannelli, L., & Zurovac, E. (2020). Political hashtag publics and counter-visuality: A case study of #fertilityday in Italy. *Information, Communication & Society*, *23*(9), 1235–1254. https://doi.org/10.1080/1369118X.2018.1555271

Woolley, S. C., & Howard, P. N. (Eds.). (2018). *Computational propaganda: Political parties, politicians, and political manipulation on social media.* Oxford University Press.

2 Curse or Cure? The Role of Algorithm in Promoting or Countering Information Disorder

Taeyoung Lee and Chenyan Jia

An Age of Information Disorder

In recent years, there has been an upsurge in scholarly interest in false or misleading information that could pollute public discourse and disturb the information ecosystem. Such growing scholarly interest is likely due to the popularity of the buzzword "fake news" and numerous real-world events globally, showcasing worrying examples of "information pollution" and its adverse impact on individuals and society (Wardle & Derakhsh, 2017, p. 5). For instance, leading up to the two most recent presidential elections in 2016 and 2020, Americans have observed so-called fake news stories circulating online; a considerable amount of them, at least widespread during 2016, turned out to be attributed to Russian trolls who attempted to manipulate the US election (Jamieson, 2018). Americans also witnessed a series of violent events that false information might have triggered such as "Pizzagate" (false information that Hillary Clinton had been involved in a child-sex ring in a DC pizzeria led a man to open fire) (Lee, 2018a) and the January 6 insurrection, also known as "Stop the Steal" rally (unsubstantiated claims of voter fraud promoted by Donald Trump to seek to overturn his loss in the 2020 presidential election led to a violent insurrection at the US Capitol) (Berlinski et al., 2021). The Brexit Referendum in the United Kingdom is another notable example that Western democracies have suffered from falsehoods prevalent in public discourse (Kucharski, 2016). Considering such a series of events, it is not surprising that the Collins Dictionary chose "fake news" as its 2017 word of the year (Lee, 2018a).

The widespread false information and its detrimental societal effects, however, are not a Western-specific phenomenon. Rather, those are more like phenomena observed across the globe, from East and Southeast Asian countries (e.g., China, Myanmar, Indonesia) to Global South including countries in South America (e.g., Brazil and Mexico) and Africa (e.g., Kenya, Nigeria and South Africa) (Carson & Fallon, 2021; Wasserman & Madrid-Morales, 2019). Furthermore, as with the rise of the COVID-19 pandemic, the flow of false or misleading information has become an issue of deep global concern because when people feel uncertain about an unknown event, such

DOI: 10.4324/9781003299936-2

information could lead to misperceptions about scientific facts, undermining the pandemic response efforts worldwide (Lee et al., 2022). As such, countries around the world had to battle against false information along with the novel virus (Smith & Perry, 2021; WHO, 2020).

Not surprisingly though, the spread of false information and even the concept of fake news are not new but have been persistent for a long time (Lee, 2018b). And there are at least two things that make addressing the current phenomena more challenging than those in the past. Firstly, as the term "fake news" has become a global buzzword, it has been also used as a convenient label describing any kind of false or misleading information. This is problematic because the word cannot fully capture the complexity of the information pollution: some do not take the form of news stories (e.g., misleading images, memes or doctored videos), or some are not completely false but present true and false information together, for example. More problematic is that the term has been politically weaponized to delegitimize and attack journalism (Egelhofer & Lecheler, 2019). Furthermore, despite peoples' mounting concerns over the harmful effects of fake news (Lee et al., 2022), exposure to fake news is known to be rare and its actual effects on real-world events such as elections are not clear (Nyhan, 2020). Secondly, what is new in the recent phenomena is the ease of creating low-quality information and the speed and reach of such information due to social media and advanced information technologies. Such technologies—data-driven algorithms, artificial intelligence (AI) and bots, to name a few—are likely to compound the adverse effects of false or low-quality information especially when those are exploited by malicious actors (Giansiracusa, 2021; Wang et al., 2018).

What Is Information Disorder?

In response to such challenges, Wardle and Derakhsh (2017) provided a useful, conceptual framework: "information disorder." According to the authors, information disorder can be categorized into three types based on falseness and intent to harm—*misinformation, disinformation* and *mal-information*—although the terms are often used interchangeably with some fluid and overlapping definitions (Guess & Lyons, 2020), and the distinction, especially between misinformation and disinformation, is more complex in reality.

Misinformation refers to content that is false but not intended to harm, ranging from unintentional mistakes such as misleading quotes and inaccurate image captions to satire when it is taken seriously (Wardle, 2018b). *Disinformation* is similar to misinformation in its falsity but different in its intent to harm. Put differently, disinformation is false information deliberately designed or disseminated to cause harm by deceiving others, which includes fabricated or manipulated audio/visual content and intentionally created conspiracy theories/rumors. The major motivations behind creating or spreading disinformation are political influence (either foreign or domestic), financial gain, and psychological or social reasons (e.g., to cultivate political cynicism or distrust among people) (Wardle, 2018a). However, when people share disinformation with others not realizing it is false, it turns into misinformation (Wardle, 2020). For this reason, disinformation is often regarded as the subset of misinformation (Guess & Lyons, 2020; Tucker et al., 2018).

Mal-information, as with disinformation, is intended to harm but is likely genuine and truthful information. It includes deliberate publication of private or confidential information such as revenge porn and the Russian leak of hacked emails from the Hilary Clinton campaign (Wardle, 2018a, 2018b). Another type of information disorder that Wardle and Derakhsh (2017) did not categorize but is worth noting is propaganda. Propaganda refers to information created and distributed to persuade others often with a hidden agenda or to disparage opposing viewpoints (Tucker et al., 2018; Wardle, 2018a). Given that either true or false information is used for propaganda, it could be disinformation or mal-information, depending on its falseness.

The information disorder framework is useful in that it allows researchers to examine various types of problematic information above and beyond fake news and how the problems can be exacerbated by the intention of actors and computational assistance. This also helps to come up with realistic solutions or interventions based on the nature of the information of interest. In this light, employing that framework, this chapter reviews the literature on various types of information disorder and how the aforementioned technologies, especially algorithms, contribute to information disorder in either positive or negative ways. More specifically, through the comprehensive review of literature from diverse areas including but not limited to communication, information studies, computer science and political science, this chapter discusses the roles that algorithms, which "form the core of an information architecture" (Peeters & Schuilenburg, 2020, p. 2), play in producing and promoting as well as countering information disorder. In doing so, we propose potential and feasible interventions, ranging from regulating algorithms to using algorithms as part of the solutions, as scholars suggest (e.g., Lazer et al., 2018). The interventions include detecting mis/disinformation, moderating undesirable content and promoting quality information through content curation.

Blaming It on Algorithms

As the internet and social media are the primary gateways to access information and means of managing everyday practices for many people (Wilson, 2017), there has been a growing awareness of algorithms imperative to the internet infrastructure (Gran et al., 2021; Proferes, 2017; Rader & Gray, 2015). Even individuals who cannot describe what algorithms are and how those work might have heard that due to algorithms used by social media platforms such as Facebook and Twitter; they cannot see every post their friends upload or share. However, not many people actually know about algorithms, not only about what the word means but also about how much their everyday life, including getting and processing information, is governed and controlled by algorithms.

According to Gillespie (2014), algorithms refer to "encoded procedures for transforming input data into a desired output, based on specified calculations" (p. 167). Simply put, algorithms are a set of instructions or steps that a computer performs to solve a problem or undertake a task (Finn, 2017; Wardle & Derakhsh, 2017). As Wilson (2017) noted, algorithms are central to our information architecture and "the ways communication and information (including the relational) are located, retrieved, filtered, presented and/or prevented" in online spaces (p. 140). Specifically, algorithms built into social media platforms filter and prioritize particular types of information (Bozdag, 2013). In this way, algorithms can even promote false or harmful information so that such information could go viral and influence people's perception or way of seeing the world (Krasmann, 2020; Lor, 2018). AI-based algorithms also contribute to information disorder by creating realistic and convincing fake content (Giansiracusa, 2021). These are the reasons why algorithms are often blamed as the culprit of the current information pollution. The roles that algorithms play in creating and aggravating information disorder are discussed in more detail in the following sections.

The Role of Algorithms in Amplifying Information Disorder

According to the literature, algorithms are known to amplify information disorder in various ways. First and foremost, algorithms can spread false and/ or harmful information easily and broadly. In particular, bots, or automated programs that are created from sets of algorithms for disseminating particular messages, tend to contribute to the visibility of certain messages by sharing them in high volume (Pomerantsev, 2019). Indeed, Shao and colleagues (2017) supported such findings by analyzing false claims spreading on Twitter during and following the 2016 US presidential election campaign. The authors found that accounts that actively spread false information including fake news stories were more likely to be bots than regular social media users. Bessi and Ferrara (2016) also found that Twitter bots represented 14% of active users and generated 20% of all tweets during the same election.

Bots might effectively spread information disorder not only because of the volume of information they can distribute but also because they can induce "conformity among human agents who would then further distribute their messages" (Wardle & Derakhshan, 2017, p. 37). Bots that look and act like real people can create "the illusion of large-scale consensus" (Woolley & Howard, 2017, p. 6) as if many individuals independently endorse the same piece of information (Ratkiewicz et al., 2011). In line with this, Wang et al. (2018) presented the hypothetical scenario that intelligent bots massively disseminate deceptive information on Twitter by infecting as many human users as possible.

Algorithms also play a significant role in amplifying information disorder by distributing particular information to specific groups of people. This so-called micro-targeting, which is a business model mainly used for the purpose of advertising (Maréchal & Biddle, 2020), is employed to disseminate false or harmful information as well. Algorithms record everything we do online and use such information to spread disinformation or mal-information to targeted audiences (Hendrix & Carroll, 2017; Pomerantsev, 2019). It is known that agents tend to target influential users (Shao et al., 2017) or groups of people that are highly receptive to a particular message (Wardle & Derakhshan, 2017). If those targeted audiences are influenced by the message, they are likely to share it on their networks, contributing to its propagation. Citing examples of YouTube that provides recommendations on what video to watch next, Bontridder and Poullet (2021) also pointed out that algorithms based on micro-targeting can directly amplify false information.

Last but not least, algorithms amplify information disorder by fostering an information environment vulnerable to falsehoods as well. Algorithms that further recommend additional content based on individuals' online history could influence their selection process by promoting content that confirms their existing beliefs or preferences. This could reduce content diversity people can consume and confine them to so-called echo chambers (Cinelli et al., 2020; Schmidt et al., 2017). In such digital spaces, individuals get easily susceptible to unsubstantiated or harmful content because they might become less skeptical or critical about the content they come across. This is also related to the aforementioned illusion of consensus and micro-targeting. If carefully targeted people are exposed to false information that looks real in an environment where they are surrounded by like-minded others, they are more likely to accept the information and share it with no doubt (Bontridder & Poullet, 2021).

The Role of Algorithms in Creating Information Disorder

Algorithms contribute to the polluted flow of information online not only by amplifying false or harmful information already created but also by producing disingenuous content realistically and convincingly. In the light of the fake news phenomenon that has become a deep societal concern, it is troubling that AI can write headlines, select pictures for the article and even write entire articles similar to those written by humans (Giansiracusa, 2021). As an example, in June 2020, Microsoft's MSN announced that dozens of news production workers would be replaced with AI as their work can be performed by algorithms (Baker, 2020). Even if the automated headlines are not perfect, this means fake headlines mimicking real news headlines can be automatically written using AI-based algorithms. Further, algorithms turned out to be capable of even writing quite sophisticated articles in a realistic format. In a novel study, Kreps and McCain (2019) examined whether AI could write convincing news stories about complicated foreign policy issues using non-factual information. They found that the majority of the readers perceived AI-generated news stories to be credible, and one in four answered they were willing to share those articles. This finding is worrisome, suggesting that algorithms can be used for generating fake news stories that could sound convincing.

The content that algorithms can create, however, is not limited to textual information. AI techniques can also create fake visual content including images, graphics and videos. As Akers et al. (2018) noted, digital tools like Photoshop made it possible to manipulate images even without sophisticated skills. In addition, deepfakes, which refer to extremely realistic videos created using deep learning algorithms, pose even more serious threats to the information ecosystem (Paris & Donovan, 2019). Compounding the fake news phenomenon, deepfakes have constituted an important part of the information disorder (Maher, 2022).

Deepfakes are troubling in that they could depict events that never happened and be used and interpreted as evidence (Paris & Donovan, 2019). Scholars have warned that deepfakes can be abused to hurt individuals (e.g., revenge porn, blackmail and cyberbullying) and to distort reality and manipulate public discourse (e.g., political sabotage, terrorist propaganda, fake video evidence in courts and fake news) (Maras & Alexandrou, 2019; Westerlund, 2019). Moreover, the hyperrealism of deepfakes offers a heuristic cue that leads people to believe the audio/video manipulation and spread the content (Sundar et al., 2021). As suggested by Vaccari and Chadwick's (2020) research, people are also more likely to feel uncertain when seeing deepfakes, and such uncertainty, in turn, undermines their trust in news media. But the biggest challenge deepfakes might pose is that they can lead to "information apocalypse" or "reality apathy," the perception that everything could be deception (Westerlund, 2019).

Fighting Against Information Disorder

While some scholars blame algorithms for creating and amplifying mis/disinformation, other scholars argue that AI may have some, but limited, potential to attenuate the information disorder such as detecting mis/disinformation (e.g., Shu et al., 2017) and automating the process of content moderation (e.g., Gillespie, 2020; Wang, 2021). Although creating effective algorithms with high accuracy faces many challenges as mis/disinformation content evolves rapidly (Pennycook & Rand, 2021), the mechanism of algorithms offers the potential benefit to catch large scale of false or harmful information, especially on social media (Zhou & Zafarani, 2020). As scholars and practitioners continue to improve the accuracy of misinformation detection algorithms and content moderation algorithms, it is promising that algorithms can, to some extent, help mitigate the dissemination of information disorder.

The Role of Algorithms in Detecting Information Disorder

In recent years, AI becomes an increasingly crucial tool to prevent the dissemination of false or misleading information. On the one hand, the application of algorithms allows scaling the work of human fact-checkers. For instance, social media platforms such as Facebook have adopted AI systems to detect duplications of information that has been flagged as mis/disinformation by independent fact-checkers (Sumbaly et al., 2020). Algorithms are also capable of detecting variations of such information as the same piece of mis/disinformation may appear in slightly different forms such as cropped images or images modified with a filter (Sumbaly et al., 2020). On the other hand, algorithms offer possible approaches to real-time news verification and interventions. Some social media companies have employed the detection results of algorithms to down-rank the content classified as problematic by algorithms so that users are less likely to see the false or harmful information (Pennycook & Rand, 2021) or put warning labels on such content to increase users' attention and reduce their sharing intention (Yaqub et al., 2020).

Many researchers and practitioners have developed various detection algorithms leveraging machine learning, natural language processing and network-based methods to detect false and misleading information (Horne & Adali, 2017; Hosseinimotlagh & Papalexakis, 2018). Zhou and Zafarani (2020) summarize four methods of automatic detection: (1) *knowledge-based* methods which detect mis/disinformation by verifying the truthfulness of statements within the news content (Shu et al., 2017); (2) *style-based* methods which distinguish the linguistic features and characteristics of accurate from inaccurate information such as emotions, title structure and the use of proper nouns (e.g., Horne & Adali, 2017; Hosseinimotlagh & Papalexakis, 2018); (3) *propagation-based* methods which detect mis/disinformation based on how users spread such information (i.e., the pattern of misinformation dissemination); (4) *source-based* methods which detect false or misleading information by assessing the credibility of news sources including authors and publishers.

In order to achieve highly accurate models, enormous efforts have been spent on cultivating large-scale datasets and using sophisticated techniques to train algorithms. Most existing automatic methods of detecting fake news are supervised, which require large-scale annotated datasets such as LIAR (Wang, 2017) and BuzzFeedNews (Potthast et al., 2018). An alternative automatic detection method is unsupervised. For example, Yang et al. (2019) found that their unsupervised model, which extracts users' opinions, credibility and engagement on social media, was able to outperform previous unsupervised detection models.

Even though researchers have endeavored to achieve higher accuracy and efficacy of detection algorithms, it is worth noting that the current detection algorithms have certain limitations. Firstly, due to the constantly changing nature of fake news, the detection methods may be outdated in a short period of time as the misinformation content evolves rapidly (Ruchansky et al., 2017). Secondly, the classification of true and false is a complicated task, which is not always black and white. Even professional fact-checkers may disagree on the classification of information (Pennycook & Rand, 2021). Therefore, algorithms run the risk of making errors or making biased judgments against specific groups depending on how they were trained (Barocas & Selbst, 2016).

The Role of Algorithms in Content Moderation

In addition to mis/disinformation detection, AI and automation are also increasingly used in the content moderation processes to address some ills of online discussions and the problem of mal-information (Wang, 2021). The use of uncivil content including problematic and offensive content has become a common problem on online networks. Social media platforms and news organizations rely on moderators to review and screen out information that does not align with their community standards (Wojcieszak et al., 2021), delete malicious content or penalize users for abusive behaviors (Almerekhi et al., 2020). Given the sheer number of offensive and toxic languages on online networks nowadays, human interventions are oftentimes not scalable and may include those human moderators' own biases (Masullo et al., 2020).

For this reason, AI is increasingly used to the online content moderation process. AI can help moderate a variety of harmful content and mal-information such as hate speech, pornography, defamatory posts or uncivil discussions (Wojcieszak et al., 2021). AI moderators trained with large datasets may provide a more cost-effectively moderation of harmful online content compared with human moderators (Cambridge Consultants, 2019). In its infancy, AI was mostly used to assist human moderators such as filtering unclear content that needs to evaluate or assist journalists in data retrieval and sourcing articles (Risch & Krestel, 2018; Wojcieszak et al., 2021). As content moderation algorithms continue to advance and the training datasets continue to expand, some online platforms including Twitter and YouTube started using AI as a primary source to identify and remove inappropriate comments, replacing human moderators (Gillespie, 2020; Magalhães & Katzenbach, 2020; Roberts, 2020). For instance, a report YouTube published in 2020 shows that 98% of the videos removed for violent extremism are flagged by algorithms (Gorwa et al., 2020).

Many organizations follow an online content moderation workflow, which consists of *pre-moderation* (i.e., when the uploaded content is moderated prior to the publication) and *post-moderation* (i.e., when the content is moderated after it has been published) (Cambridge Consultants, 2019). Algorithms can play important roles in both pre- and post-content moderation stages respectively. In the *pre-moderation* stage, AI can be implemented to synthesize training data to improve pre-moderation performance. For instance, AI techniques such as generative adversarial networks (GANs) can be used to generate new training data in different formats such as images, video, audio or text. These newly generated training data can supplement the existing examples of harmful content to train a better AI-based moderation system (e.g., Zhu et al., 2017). AI moderation techniques can also be used in the *pre-moderation* stage to flag the content that requires to be reviewed by humans or to provide valuable context such as the users' metadata to assist human moderators' decisions. In the *post-moderation* stage when the content is moderated after the publication but requires a second review upon appeal, AI can also assist human moderators to make decisions. In addition, AI techniques can suggest a rewording that replaces the harmful words while preserving the sentiments (Santos et al., 2018).

The optimism toward automated content moderation is often justified as a response to scale. However, some scholars have expressed their concerns about the pitfalls and challenges of AI-enabled content moderation. Firstly, AI-based content moderations are prone to make errors as content moderation is a complex task (Cambridge Consultants, 2019). Gillespie (2020) argues that some social media companies may overstate the successful rate of their automated moderation. Secondly, it is difficult for automated content moderation to account for the context, subtlety, sarcasm and subcultural meaning of particular content (Duarte et al., 2018; Gillespie, 2020). As platforms' content moderation policies often adapt over time (Sinnreich, 2018), algorithms need to iterate frequently in response to the rapid evolution of online content and adapting policies. Thirdly, content classifiers may be more or less favorable to content associated with protected classes (e.g., gender, race, religion and disability) and thus may have unequal impacts on different populations (Gorwa et al., 2020).

Possible Solutions

With advanced natural language processing and machine learning techniques, algorithms become ubiquitous in the contemporary media environment. In the era of unprecedented information disorder, algorithms can be seen as both a blessing and a curse. On the one hand, algorithms are blamed for negatively affecting democratic political discussion (Bessi & Ferrara, 2016), spreading more mis/disinformation or extreme viewpoints (Ribeiro et al., 2020; Woolley & Howard, 2016) and minimizing diverse exposure to news content (Pariser, 2011). On the other hand, automation can release some of the burdens of humans as well as enable scalable detection of false and harmful information detection and moderation at a high speed (Gillespie, 2020). Instead of blaming AI as culprits for spreading false or harmful information or over-romanticizing

AI's potential for mitigating information disorder, perhaps a better way is to come up with feasible solutions to standardize the development of algorithms and regulate the usage of algorithms.

Regulating Algorithms

The growing needs of algorithms in the information dissemination process give rise to a new social ordering known as algorithmic regulation (Yeung, 2018). There are a number of critical issues for algorithmic regulation including accountability (i.e., reporting standards backed by sanctions) and transparency (i.e., allowing for external scrutiny) (Lodge & Mennicken, 2017). Diakopoulos (2015) suggests that algorithmic accountability must consider the fact that algorithms are created by humans so that human influences should be embedded into the development of algorithms including training data, determining criteria and interpretation. In other words, humans still should be the one to make higher-level decisions. Lodge and Mennicken (2017) also suggest that algorithm should not be programed to make ethical choices. It is hard for algorithms to accommodate diverse social values such as fairness, nuance and context due to their underlying mechanisms (Lee, 2018b). Thus, humans should make clear criteria when training a content moderation algorithm and intervene timely to reduce the error rate of algorithms.

Transparency is also important to bear on algorithmic power. To ensure transparency, both government regulation and the self-regulation of platforms are needed (Lazer et al., 2018). Similar to other areas, the government needs to impose algorithm-related transparency policies so as to compel disclosure (Fung et al., 2007). It is also necessary for platforms to self-regulate and provide a transparent report of developing and using algorithms. Google's transparency report is a good example, which indicates how often it removes information and discloses their actions to the governments (Diakopoulos, 2015). Persily (2021) proposes a so-called Platform Transparency and Accountability Act, which intends to design a data sharing program that protects user privacy and ensures independent research on platform data. The sharing of datasets applicable to identifying harmful content can help create and maintain standards between platforms and moderation service providers (Cambridge Consultants, 2019). UK government's recent report shows that the shared dataset held by public institutions such as BBC not only can keep the data up to date with evolving categories of harmful content but can also benefit the society (GOV.UK., 2017).

Alongside regulation enacted by governments and social media platforms, journalists and scholars can also play crucial roles in helping the public to learn the critical use of various news-related algorithms as well as the downsides of such technologies. For instance, Yadlin-Segal and Oppenheim (2021) suggest that journalists not only can help improve the digital literacy of the general public by introducing the pros and cons of deepfakes algorithms but can develop the possible positive potential of using deepfakes technology as well. Computer scientists and social scientists who audit computer algorithms or conduct studies on how algorithms shape public opinions could also collaborate with algorithms developers and provide academic insights (Lazer et al., 2018; Woolley & Howard, 2016).

Creating and Using Algorithms for Public Good

In recent years, there have been substantial debates on how to create algorithms for the public good. The first approach is to reduce bias in automated systems. Although early scholars hold a prospect of algorithm neutrality, automated systems have been increasingly recognized as reflecting existing societal biases and even introducing a new bias (Leppänen et al., 2020; Selbst et al., 2019). A growing body of scholarship has discussed the potential for automated systems to make unfair or discriminatory decisions against a certain group of people (Gorwa et al., 2020). Bias in algorithmic techniques and autonomous systems is often caused by the bias in the training dataset and the language models (Danks & London, 2017; Leppänen et al., 2020). Thus, in order to create algorithms with potentially less bias, scholars and programmers should endeavor to create and use more balanced, fair and unbiased training datasets and mitigate bias in language models (Liu et al., 2021, 2022).

The second approach is to create and use algorithms that can promote socially positive online engagement. For instance, chatbots can be used to discourage users from posting potentially harmful content by prompting them to rethink before posting harmful or offensive content (Cambridge Consultants, 2019). Other AI techniques can be also leveraged to suggest less harmful or offensive languages, which is an alternative to nudge users to post less negative content. One recent study uses unsupervised text style transfer to reparse an offensive sentence into a civil version while preserving the most relevant information (Santos et al., 2018). Such algorithms should be further tested and have the potential to be applied to practice.

Conclusion

There have been growing concerns about information disorder in recent years. While the problem of false or harmful information is not new, the problem in the digitally connected world has presented an unprecedented challenge in terms of its reach and consequences. In particular, algorithms are known to add an increased level of complexity to the issue by playing ambivalent roles. As discussed earlier, algorithms are capable of creating, spreading and amplifying various forms of information disorder, which exacerbates the problem. At the same time, however, algorithms can also be part of the solution that mitigates the problem by detecting such information and helping content moderation decisions. However, algorithmic solutions cannot be the cure-all. As

Lazer and colleagues (2018) suggested, to fix the problem of information disorder, a "new system of safeguard" (p. 1095) is imperative, which not only utilizes algorithms and AI to mitigate information disorder but also empowers individuals to be less susceptible to information pollution through multidisciplinary effort.

References

Ahmad, I., Yousaf, M., Yousaf, S., & Ahmad, M. O. (2020). Fake news detection using machine learning ensemble methods. *Complexity*. 2020, 1–11.

Akers, J., Bansal, G., Cadamuro, G., Chen, C., Chen, Q., Lin, L., . . . Roesner, F. (2018). Technology-enabled disinformation: Summary, lessons, and recommendations. *arXiv preprint arXiv:1812.09383*.

Almerekhi, H., Kwak, H., & Jansen, B. (2020). Statistical modeling of harassment against Reddit moderators. *Companion Proceedings of the Web Conference*, 122–123. doi:10.1145/3366424.3382729

Baker, G. (2020, May 29). Microsoft is cutting dozens of MSN news production workers and replacing them with artificial intelligence. *Seattle Times*. www.seattletimes.com/business/local-business/microsoft-is-cutting-dozens-of-msn-news-production-workers-and-replacing-them-with-artificial-intelligence/

Barocas, S., & Selbst, A. D. (2016). Big data's disparate impact. *California Law Review, 104*, 671.

Berlinski, N., Doyle, M., Guess, A. M., Levy, G., Lyons, B., Montgomery, J. M., Nyhan, B., & Reifler, J. (2021). The effects of unsubstantiated claims of voter fraud on confidence in elections. *Journal of Experimental Political Science*, 1–16. https://doi.org/10.1017/XPS.2021.18

Bessi, A., & Ferrara, E. (2016). Social bots distort the 2016 U.S. Presidential election online discussion. *First Monday, 21*(11). https://doi.org/10.5210/fm.v21i11.7090

Bontridder, N., & Poullet, Y. (2021). The role of artificial intelligence in disinformation. *Data & Policy, 3*. https://doi.org/ 10.1017/dap.2021.20

Bozdag, E. (2013). Bias in algorithmic filtering and personalization. *Ethics and Information Technology, 15*, 209–227. https://doi.org/10.1007/s10676-013-9321-6

Cambridge Consultants. (2019). Use of AI in online content moderation. Retrieved from https://www.cambridgeconsultants.com/us/insights/whitepaper/ofcom-use-ai-online-content-moderation

Carson, A., & Fallon, L. (2021). *Fighting fake news: A study of online misinformation regulation in the Asia pacific*. La Trobe University.

Cinelli, M., Morales, G. D. F., Galeazzi, A., Quattrociocchi, W., & Starnini, M. (2020). Echo chambers on social media: A comparative analysis. *arXiv preprint arXiv:2004.09603*.

Danks, D., & London, A. J. (2017). *Algorithmic bias in autonomous systems*. Proceedings of the Twenty-Sixth International Joint Conference on Artificial Intelligence, pp. 4691–4697. https://doi.org/10.24963/ijcai.2017/654

Diakopoulos, N. (2015). Algorithmic accountability: Journalistic investigation of computational power structures. *Digital Journalism, 3*(3), 398–415.

Duarte, N., Llanso, E., & Loup, A. C. (2018). Mixed messages? The limits of automated social media content analysis. *Center for Democracy & Technology*. 2017, 1-28. Retrieved from https://apo.org.au/sites/default/files/resource-files/2017-11/apo-nid240471.pdf

Egelhofer, J. L., & Lecheler, S. (2019). Fake news as a two-dimensional phenomenon: A framework and research agenda. *Annals of the International Communication Association, 43*(2), 97–116. https://doi.org/10.1080/23808985.2019.1602782

Finn, E. (2017). *What algorithms want: Imagination in the age of computing.* MIT Press.

Fung, A., Graham, M., & Weil, D. (2007). *Full disclosure: The perils and promise of transparency.* Cambridge University Press.

Giansiracusa, N. (2021). *How algorithms create and prevent fake news: Exploring the impacts of social media, deep fakes, GPT-3, and more.* Apress.

Gillespie, T. (2014). The relevance of algorithms. In T. Gillespie, P. J. Boczkowski, & K. A. Foot (Eds.), *Media technologies: Essays on communication, materiality, and society* (pp. 167–93). The MIT Press.

Gillespie, T. (2020). Content moderation, AI, and the question of scale. *Big Data & Society, 7*(2), 2053951720943234.

Gorwa, R., Binns, R., & Katzenbach, C. (2020). Algorithmic content moderation: Technical and political challenges in the automation of platform governance. *Big Data & Society, 7*(1), 2053951719897945.

GOV.UK. (2017). *Growing the artificial intelligence industry in the UK.* www.gov.uk/government/publications/growing-the-artificial-intelligence-industry-in-the-uk

Gran, A.-B., Booth, P., & Bucher, T. (2021). To be or not to be algorithm aware: A question of a new digital divide? *Information, Communication & Society, 24*(12), 1779–1796. https://doi.org/10.1080/1369118X.2020.1736124

Guess, A. M., & Lyons, B. A. (2020). Misinformation, disinformation, and online propaganda. In *Social media and democracy: The state of the field, prospects for reform* (pp. 10–33). Cambridge University Press.

Hendrix, J., & Carroll, D. (2017, May 4). Confronting a nightmare for democracy personal data, personalized media and weaponized propaganda. *Medium.* https://medium.com/@profcarroll/confronting-a-nightmare-for-democracy-5333181ca675

Horne, B. D., & Adali, S. (2017). *This just in: Fake news packs a lot in title, uses simpler, repetitive content in text body, more similar to satire than real news.* 11th International AAAI Conference on Web and Social Media.

Hosseinimotlagh, S., & Papalexakis, E. E. (2018). *Unsupervised content-based identification of fake news articles with tensor decomposition ensembles.* Proceedings of the Workshop on Misinformation and Misbehavior Mining on the Web (MIS2).

Jamieson, K. H. (2018). *Cyberwar: How Russian hackers and trolls helped elect a president.* Oxford University Press.

Krasmann, S. (2020). The logic of the surface: On the epistemology of algorithms in times of big data. *Information Communication and Society, 23*(14), 2096–2109. https://doi.org/10.1080/1369118X.2020.1726986

Kreps, S., & McCain, M. (2019, August 2). Not your father's bots: AI is making fake news look real. *Foreign Affairs.* www.foreignaffairs.com/articles/2019-08-02/not-your-fathers-bots

Kucharski, A. (2016). Study epidemiology of fake news. *Nature, 540*(7634), 525–525. https://doi.org/10.1038/540525a

Lazer, D. M., Baum, M. A., Benkler, Y., Berinsky, A. J., Greenhill, K. M., Menczer, F., ... & Zittrain, J. L. (2018). The science of fake news. *Science, 359*(6380), 1094–1096.

Lee, N. T. (2018a). Detecting racial bias in algorithms and machine learning. *Journal of Information, Communication and Ethics in Society.*

Lee, N. T. (2018b). *Perceived influence of fake news and its consequences* (Publication No. 10822316). [Master's Thesis, Indiana University]. ProQuest Dissertations and Theses Global (2074697424).

Lee, T., Johnson, T. J., & Sturm Wilkerson, H. (2022). You can't handle the lies! Exploring the role of Gamson Hypothesis in explaining third-person perceptions of being fooled by fake news and fake news sharing. *Mass Communication and Society*, 1–24. https://doi.org/10.1080/15205436.2022.2026401

Lee, T., Johnson, T. J., & Weaver, D. H. (2022). Navigating the coronavirus Infodemic: Exploring the impact of need for orientation, epistemic beliefs and type of media use on knowledge and misperception about COVID-19. *Mass Communication and Society*, 1–26. https://doi.org/10.1080/15205436.2022.2046103

Leppänen, L., Tuulonen, H., & Sirén-Heikel, S. (2020). Automated journalism as a source of and a diagnostic device for bias in reporting. *Media and Communication*, *8*(3), 39–49. https://doi.org/10.17645/mac.v8i3.3022

Liu, R., Jia, C., Wei, J., Xu, G., & Vosoughi, S. (2022). Quantifying and alleviating political bias in language models. *Artificial Intelligence*, *304*, 103654.

Liu, R., Jia, C., Wei, J., Xu, G., Wang, L., & Vosoughi, S. (2021). Mitigating political bias in language models through reinforced calibration. *Proceedings of the AAAI Conference on Artificial Intelligence*, *35*, 14857–14866.

Lodge, M., & Mennicken, A. (2017). The importance of regulation of and by algorithm. *Algorithmic Regulation*, *2*.

Lor, P. J. (2018). Democracy, information, and libraries in a time of post-truth discourse. *Library Management*, 39(5), 307–321. https://doi.org/10.1108/LM-06-2017-0061.

Magalhães, J. C., & Katzenbach, C. (2020). Coronavirus and the frailness of platform governance. *Internet Policy Review*, *9*.

Maher, S. (2022). Deep fakes: Seeing and not believing. In M. Filimowicz (Ed.), *Algorithms and society: Deep fakes* (pp. 1–22). Routledge.

Maras, M. H., & Alexandrou, A. 2019. Determining authenticity of video evidence in the age of artificial intelligence and in the wake of Deepfake videos. *International Journal of Evidence & Proof*, *23*(3), 255–262. https://doi.org/10.1177/13657127 18807226

Maréchal, N., & Biddle, E. R. (2020, March 17). It's not just the content, It's the business model: Democracy's online speech challenge: A report from ranking digital rights. *New America*. www.newamerica.org/oti/reports/its-not-just-content-its-business-model/

Masullo, G. M., Riedl, M. J., & Huang, Q. E. (2020). Engagement moderation: What journalists should say to improve online discussions. *Journalism Practice*, 1–17. doi:10.1080/17512786.2020.1808858

Nyhan, B. (2020, November 6). Five myths about misinformation. *The Washington Post*. www.washingtonpost.com/outlook/five-myths/five-myths-about-misinformation/2020/11/06/b28f2e94-1ec2-11eb-90dd-abd0f7086a91_story.html

Paris, B., & Donovan, J. (2019). *Deepfakes and cheap fakes*. Data & Society. https://datasociety.net/output/deepfakes-and-cheap-fakes/

Pariser, E. (2011). *The filter bubble: How the new personalized web is changing what we read and how we think*. Penguin Books. http://rbdigital.oneclickdigital.com

Peeters, R., & Schuilenburg, M. (2020). The algorithmic society: An introduction. In M. Schuilenburg & R. Peeters (Eds.), *The algorithmic society* (pp. 1–15). Routledge.

Pennycook, G., & Rand, D. G. (2021). The psychology of fake news. *Trends in Cognitive Sciences*, *25*(5), 388–402.

Persily, N. (2021). A proposal for researcher access to platform data: The platform transparency and accountability act. *Journal of Online Trust and Safety, 1*(1).

Pomerantsev, P. (2019). *This is not propaganda: Adventures in the war against reality.* Faber & Faber.

Potthast, M., Kiesel, J., Reinartz, K., Bevendorff, J., & Stein, B. (2018). A stylometric inquiry into hyperpartisan and fake news. In *Proceedings of the 56th annual meeting of the association for computational linguistics (volume 1: Long papers)* (pp. 231–240).

Proferes, N. (2017). Information flow solipsism in an exploratory study of beliefs about Twitter. *Social Media + Society, 3*(1). https://doi.org/10.1177/2056305117698493

Rader, E., & Gray, R. (2015). Understanding user beliefs about algorithmic curation in the Facebook news feed. In *Proceedings of the 33rd annual ACM conference on human factors in computing systems—CHI "15* (pp. 173–182). ACM Press.

Ratkiewicz et al. (2011). *Detecting and tracking political abuse in social media.* Proceedings of the Fifth International AAAI Conference on Weblogs and Social Media. www.aaai.org/ocs/index.php/ICWSM/ICWSM11/paper/view/2850

Ribeiro, M. H., Ottoni, R., West, R., Almeida, V. A., & Meira Jr, W. (2020). Auditing radicalization pathways on YouTube. *In Proceedings of the 2020 conference on fairness, accountability, and transparency* (pp. 131–141).

Risch, J., & Krestel, R. (2018). Delete or not delete? Semi-automatic comment moderation for the newsroom. *In Proceedings of the first workshop on trolling, aggression and cyberbullying* (pp. 166–176). ACL.

Roberts, S. T. (2020). Fewer humans are moderating Facebook content. That's worrying. *Slate Magazine.*

Ruchansky, N., Seo, S., & Liu, Y. (2017). Csi: A hybrid deep model for fake news detection. In *Proceedings of the 2017 ACM on conference on information and knowledge management* (pp. 797–806).

Santos, C. N. D., Melnyk, I., & Padhi, I. (2018). Fighting offensive language on social media with unsupervised text style transfer. In *Proceedings of the 56th annual meeting of the association for computational linguistics (volume 2: Short papers)* (pp. 189–194).

Schmidt, A. L., Zollo, F., Del Vicario, M., Bessi, A., Scala, A., Caldarelli, G., Stanley, H. E., & Quattrociocchi, W. (2017). Anatomy of news consumption on Facebook. *Proceedings of the National Academy of Sciences, 114*(12), 3035–3039.

Selbst, A. D., Boyd, D., Friedler, S. A., Venkatasubramanian, S., & Vertesi, J. (2019). Fairness and abstraction in sociotechnical systems. In *Proceedings of the conference on fairness, accountability, and transparency* (pp. 59–68).

Shao, C., Ciampaglia, G. L., Varol, O., Flammini, A., & Menczer, F. (2017, July 24). *The spread of fake news by social bots.* https://arxiv.org/pdf/1707.07592.pdf

Shu, K., Sliva, A., Wang, S., Tang, J., & Liu, H. (2017). Fake news detection on social media: A data mining perspective. *ACM SIGKDD Explorations Newsletter, 19*(1), 22–36.

Sinnreich, A. (2018). Four crises in algorithmic governance. *Annual Review of Law and Ethics, 26*, 181–190.

Smith, R. B., Perry, M., & Smith, N. N. (2021). 'Fake news" in ASEAN: Legislative responses. *Journal of ASEAN Studies, 22*(2), 131–154.

Sumbaly, R., Miller, M., Shah, H., Xie, Y., Culatana, S. C., Khatkevich, T., . . . Jegou, H. (2020). Using AI to detect COVID19 misinformation and exploitative content. *Facebook Artificial Intelligence.* https://ai.facebook.com/blog/using-ai-to-detect-covid-19-misinformation-and-exploitative-content/

Sundar, S. S., Molina, M. D., & Cho, E. (2021). Seeing is believing: Is video modality more powerful in spreading fake news via online messaging apps? *Journal of Computer-Mediated Communication, 26*(6), 301–319. https://doi.org/10.1093/jcmc/zmab010

Tucker, J. A., Guess, A., Barberá, P., Vaccari, C., Siegel, A., Sanovich, S., Stukal, D., & Nyhan, B. (2018, March 19). Social media, political polarization, and political disinformation: A review of the scientific literature. *Political Polarization, and Political Disinformation: A Review of the Scientific Literature.* http://dx.doi.org/10.2139/ssrn.3144139

Vaccari, C., & Chadwick, A. (2020). Deepfakes and disinformation: Exploring the impact of synthetic political video on deception, uncertainty, and trust in news. *Social Media+ Society, 6*(1), 2056305120903408

Wang, P., Angarita, R., & Renna, I. (2018, April). Is this the era of misinformation yet: Combining social bots and fake news to deceive the masses. In *Companion proceedings of the web conference 2018* (pp. 1557–1561).

Wang, S. (2021). Moderating uncivil user comments by humans or machines? The effects of moderation agent on perceptions of bias and credibility in news content. *Digital Journalism,* 1–20.

Wang, W. Y. (2017). "Liar, liar pants on fire": A new benchmark dataset for fake news detection. In *Proceedings of the 55th annual meeting of the association for computational linguistics (volume 2: Short papers)* (pp. 422–426).

Wardle, C. (2018a). *Information disorder: The essential glossary. Shorenstein center on media, politics, and public policy.* Harvard Kennedy School.

Wardle, C. (2018b). The need for smarter definitions and practical, timely empirical research on information disorder. *Digital Journalism, 6*(8), 951–963. https://doi.org/10.1080/21670811.2018.1502047

Wardle, C. (2020, September 22). Understanding Information disorder. *First Draft.* Retrieved from https://firstdraftnews.org/long-form-article/understanding-information-disorder/

Wardle, C., & Derakhshan, H. (2017). Information disorder: Toward an interdisciplinary framework for research and policymaking. *Council of Europe Report,* 1–108.

Wasserman, H., & Madrid-Morales, D. (2019). An exploratory study of "fake news" and media trust in Kenya, Nigeria and South Africa. *African Journalism Studies, 40*(1), 107–123. https://doi.org/10.1080/23743670.2019.1627230

Westerlund, M. (2019). The emergence of deepfake technology: A review. *Technology Innovation Management Review, 9*(11), 40–53.

Wilson, M. (2017). Algorithms (and the) everyday. *Information, Communication & Society, 20*(1), 137–150. https://doi.org/10.1080/1369118X.2016.1200645

Wojcieszak, M., Thakur, A., Ferreira Gonçalves, J. F., Casas, A., Menchen-Trevino, E., & Boon, M. (2021). Can AI enhance people's support for online moderation and their openness to dissimilar political views? *Journal of Computer-Mediated Communication, 26*(4), 223–243.

Woolley, S. C., & Howard, P. (2016). Political communication, computational propaganda, and autonomous agents: Introduction. *International journal of Communication, 10.*

Woolley, S. C., & Howard, P. (2017). *Computational propaganda worldwide: Executive summary.* Computational Propaganda Research Project, University of Oxford.

World Health Organization. (2020). *Coronavirus disease 2019 (COVID-19) situation report—13.* WHO.

Yadlin-Segal, A., & Oppenheim, Y. (2021). Whose dystopia is it anyway? Deepfakes and social media regulation. *Convergence, 27*(1), 36–51.

Yang, S., Shu, K., Wang, S., Gu, R., Wu, F., & Liu, H. (2019). Unsupervised fake news detection on social media: A generative approach. *Proceedings of the AAAI Conference on Artificial Intelligence, 33*(01), 5644–5651. https://doi.org/10.1609/aaai.v33i01.33015644

Yaqub, W., Kakhidze, O., Brockman, M. L., Memon, N., & Patil, S. (2020). Effects of credibility indicators on social media news sharing intent. In *Proceedings of the 2020 CHI conference on human factors in computing systems* (pp. 1–14).

Yeung, K. (2018). Algorithmic regulation: A critical interrogation. *Regulation & Governance, 12*(4), 505–523.

Zhou, X., & Zafarani, R. (2020). A survey of fake news: Fundamental theories, detection methods, and opportunities. *ACM Computing Surveys (CSUR), 53*(5), 1–40.

Zhu, J. Y., Park, T., Isola, P., & Efros, A. A. (2017). Unpaired image-to-image translation using cycle-consistent adversarial networks. In *Proceedings of the IEEE international conference on computer vision* (pp. 2223–2232).

3 For the Sake of Sharing

Fake News as Memes

Raúl Rodríguez-Ferrándiz, Cande
Sánchez-Olmos and Tatiana Hidalgo-Marí

This research work has been funded by MCIN/AEI/10.13039/501100011033
and European Union NextGenerationEU/PRTR through the projects "TRIVIAL"
(PID2021-122263OBC22) and "SocialTrust" (PDC2022-133146- C22).

Introduction

Memes are one of the most significant phenomena and most notorious social
practices of digital popular culture to the point that they have become a key format to understanding certain aspects of contemporary society. Although neither
memes nor memetics are a new phenomenon, the internet has multiplied the
ability to replicate and spread surprising ideas that materialize in a multitude
of ways (by text, audio, image, animation and so on) that are typically humorous, parodic, bizarre and so on, and which have come to be known as "internet
memes." In general terms, memes are creative practices, an emphatic form of
mise-en-scène consisting of user involvement by means of an overt montage,
which does not a priori intend to confuse anyone but rather to depict a fact, to
document something that actually exists. In semiotic terms, memes can be said
to be self-referential, such that in the entirety of their meaning they represent
nothing beyond themselves. However, it is clear that they can proceed to form,
in the manner of a collage, a blend of pieces that intertextually refer to people,
events, physical places, moments, statements and existing facts outside of the
meme.

But what if we could show that fake news is rife with strategies and
dynamics related to other memetic content? Fake news (which is not a new
phenomenon but just as with memes has been strengthened to extraordinary
degree by the proliferation of the internet) falsely depicts the state of things
in the world or transmits such states in a deceitful way, placing those who
receive and believe it in danger, a danger that is at the very least epistemic in
nature. Our hypothesis is to consider that, in current digital culture, fake news
can be legitimately analyzed through memetics. This chapter therefore seeks
to provide a critical overview of memetic culture: if it can be shown that the
replication, adaptation and spread of fake news adopts not only the *look* of

DOI: 10.4324/9781003299936-3

meme but also the *allure* of a meme, this could have more alarming social and political implications than those usually attributed to memes in terms of their being considered pieces of digital popular culture.

Certainly, the prevailing idea is that in the digital age memes help to prolong the carnivalesque, caricaturesque culture of providing a humorous critique of power (different powers), of the kind described by Bakhtin in the 1930s and 1940s (Bakhtin, 1981, 1984). It is an empowerment that comes from the bottom up, based on intertextuality, polyphony and a productivity that is separate from the market, and even runs against it (as copyright is sometimes breached), and which has come to be known in modern times as "participatory culture" (Jenkins et al., 2013), such that the meme "belongs to the people," "with no commercial interest involved" (Danung & Holloway-Attaway, 2008). Along these lines, Shifman (2014, pp. 151 et seq.) interpreted memetic practices as an epiphenomenon of globalization, not as a resource of homogenization (the negative aspect that is often attributed to globalization in terms of its effect on culture), but rather as a way of emphasizing the singular nature of the narratives of local cultures, and wrote of *user-generated globalization*: "a process in which memes are translated, customized, and distributed across the globe by ordinary internet users."

Our work investigates the possibilities of applying an interpretative framework of a similar kind to that used to explain and analyze memes, particular internet memes, to the viral spread of fake news. This category jump that we propose is a considerable one: an occurrence or an ingenious idea; a catchy phrase or saying; a challenge that involves a funny or ridiculous performance; a tune that has a dance associated with it; an evidently manipulated photo; a saying, intended as caricature or intended to shock, particularly when attributed to a pet, would all seem to have little to do with fake news.

We will first analyze what features identify, describe and analyze the memetics in memes as a practice of digital popular culture in order to explain how the physiognomy of fake news has changed depending on the history of the media and political communication, so as to observe whether a convergence or coming together of the two dynamics is possible and reasonable.

Literature Review: From Memes to Internet Memes

As is well known, in a chapter of his famous book *The Selfish Gene*, Richard Dawkins (2006 [1976]) extrapolated qualities that he had identified in genes to cultural anthropology. According to Dawkins, examples of memes range from "tunes, ideas, catch-phrases, clothes, fashions, ways of making pots or of building arches" (p. 192) to the idea of life after death, or the concept of an all-powerful god, for example, or a scientific idea such as the evolution of species. New memes can displace or abolish previous memes, or transform them, adapting them to different circumstances to give them a longer, more fertile life. Regardless, memes can be attributed the purpose of lingering, of remaining active in a no-holds-barred competition. It is why memes are described as *selfish* and *ruthless* by Dawkins in the same way as genes.

After Dawkins, many authors focused on what was in principle a marginal offshoot of this theory, splitting off under the name "memetics," and the internet era has led to unheralded growth of the concept. The term "memetics" was coined by Hans-Cees Speel in 1995. According to Heylighen and Chielens (2009, pp. 1–2), a meme is an "information pattern, held in an individual's memory, which is capable of being copied to another individual's memory," and memetics is "the theoretical and empirical science that studies the replication, spread and evolution of memes." The authors define the three properties that Dawkins extrapolated from genes as follows: longevity, the duration that an individual replicator survives; fecundity, the speed of reproduction of a replicator, as measured by the number of copies made per time unit; and copying-fidelity, the degree to which a replicator is accurately reproduced. They also highlighted the metaphor of the meme's contagion, which resembles an infectious virus more than a gene (which, obviously, is not contagious but is transferred from parents to children) (Heylighen & Chielens, 2009, pp. 1–2), and wrote of "idea viruses" or "thought contagion," as occurs with catchy tunes, or online purchase recommendations, which lead to a chain of contagion.

Much of the recent research into memes is clearly justified by and the result of the remarkable acceleration of the memetic fabric of digital culture due to the expansion of the internet first and then to social media, in its 2.0 iteration. Internet memes are "a popular term for describing the rapid uptake and spread of a particular idea presented as a written text, image, language 'move,' or some other unit of cultural 'stuff'" (Knobel & Lankshear, 2007, p. 202). In a more recent article, the same authors specify that memes are "online artefacts made up of so many different kinds (and degrees) of innovative riffs around some (often recent) originating event or other artefact" (Lankshear & Knobel, 2019, p. 43). In general terms, several authors coincide in their definitions of memes by highlighting that they are multimodal texts with varying degrees of complexity relating to popular culture and are created and transformed by users, who in turn circulate them through a range of digital channels in a context of technologically mediated communication (Davison, 2012; Dynel, 2016; Laineste & Voolaid, 2016; Milner, 2016; Shifman, 2013). Some authors highlight the characteristic of humor (Davison, 2012; Knobel & Lankshear, 2007), others the capacity of memetics as a social practice (Milner, 2016) capable of generating a memorable experience in the creative and interpretative processes in the context of a participatory culture (Shifman, 2011, 2013, p. 214) and the importance of intertextuality (Knobel & Lankshear, 2007; Laineste & Voolaid, 2016).

Specific categories of memes have been addressed, such as YouTube videos (Burgess & Green, 2009; Jenkins et al., 2013), the importance of sound and music in memetics (Sánchez-Olmos & Viñuela, 2017, 2021), fake quotations that go viral (McArdle, 2011), LOLCats (Dynel, 2016), image macro memes

(García Huerta, 2014; Yus, 2018), and the like, and an analysis has even been made of memetics as applied to local hoaxes (Rodríguez-Ferrándiz et al., 2021).

Viewed as a whole, these studies focus on the propagation of highly popular and somewhat trivial digital texts with high capacity for reproduction, such as jokes, quotes, rumors, photos and videos, many of which have obviously been manipulated to provoke a reaction, and which are shared online. Specific examples of internet memes mentioned by specialists range from the first emoticons, such as the wink: ;-), to the picture of Morpheus in the first instalment of *The Matrix* with the overlaid text "What If I told you" (see Figure 3.1), and from the fan-made video of Britney Spears in 2007 (Crocker: "Leave Britney Alone!," Shifman, 2014, pp. 42–49) to the Kanye West's interruption to the 2009 MTV Award ceremony for Best Video by a Female Artist to Taylor Swift (West: "Imma Let You Finish," Milner, 2016, pp. 11–18) to argue that Beyoncé deserved to win for her video of *Single Ladies*, as well as the dubbed or subtitled clip of the conversation between Hitler and his generals in the film *Downfall* (Oliver Hirschbiegel, 2004), for hundreds of different reasons, which is analyzed by Shifman (2011), or the video of *Gangnam Style* by Psy. Some memes are ironically self-referential, as can be seen in the third variation of the meme from *The Matrix* (Figure 3.1) and the last variation of the meme from the TV series *Game of Thrones* (Figure 3.2).

It seems that the humorous ingredient of memes is a necessary, though not sufficient, condition for them to be characterized as such. Fake news, however, has no such requirement of humor. On the contrary, it could be said that humor functions as an indicator of "fictionality" that could ruin the aim of fake news from the outset, in the meaning of the term that has become so widespread in recent years: to deceive through the fabrication of completely invented news articles or through the misrepresentation of real events when

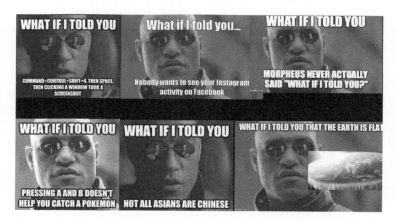

Figure 3.1 Collage of memes from *The Matrix* franchise

Figure 3.2 Collage of memes from the character Eddard "Ned" Stark from the HBO series *Game of Thrones*

reporting them in order to gain political or economic advantage. But is fake news completely separate from satire, parody or humor?

Fake News: First as Farce, Then as Tragedy

Fake news has been described as "news articles that are intentionally and veri-fiably false and could mislead readers" (Allcott & Gentzkow, 2017), with a nature that is always "misleading by design" (Gelfert, 2018, p. 108). The com-pound word "fake news" was chosen as word of the year in 2017 by the *Collins Dictionary* and the *American Dialect Society* alike, among others. They both specify that its inclusion was due to the fact that its use spread rapidly and its occurrence in public discourse multiplied as a result of the campaign that led to the referendum on Brexit in the United Kingdom (June 2016) and the presidential election campaign in the United States that led to the victory of Donald Trump in November 2016.

Certainly, the expression "fake news" is not new and dates back to the early 20th century (McNair, 2018) and related to deceitful manipulations and complete inventions of news by the more sensationalist and biased press. However, in the early 21st century, the term began to gain new notoriety, asso-ciated with its explicit appearance on TV programs parodying the news that were highly successful with audiences, such as *The Daily Show* (1999–2015) and *The Colbert Report* (2005–2014) on the US channel *Comedy Central*. The same can be said of satirical publications such as *The Onion*, parody-based columns such as "The Borowitz Report" in *The New Yorker*, or even "The Weekend Update," a segment on NBC's *Saturday Night Live*. All these explicitly pseudo-informative formats and content were described as "fake news" programs or sections and were treated as such in the academic literature that analyzed them in the early years of the 21st century (Baym, 2005; Holt, 2007; Day & Thompson, 2012; Berkowitz & Schwartz, 2016).

In one example from May 2022, "The Borowitz Report" in *The New Yorker*, which preventively states the section is "Satire" and "Not the news," included the following among its fake news items: "Trump fears Putin is too distracted by Ukraine to help him with 2024 campaign" (February 2022) and "Twitter in chaos after the Elon Musk who offered to buy it turns out to be a bot" (May 2022).

Berkowitz and Schwartz (2016) claimed that comedic fake news, unlike online fake news, is "steeped in strong exaggeration that blatantly and explicitly signals its comedic intent" (p. 3). However, online versions of fake news "avoid the slapstick and clowning, turning instead to the 'hyper-real' where both text presentations and on-screen delivery are relatively realistic" (p. 3). Researchers have also identified how comedic satirical fake news can also have negative effects when articles originating on these websites are retweeted and shared on Twitter and Facebook feeds, where they look more realistic and can be misunderstood as factual (Allcott & Gentzkow, 2017).

Indeed, in 2012, the official newspaper of the Chinese Communist Party, the *People's Daily*, included in its English-language version the news that *The Onion* had declared the North Korean leader Kim Jong-un "the sexiest man in the world." The *People's Daily* took it so seriously that it accompanied its article with 55 photographs of the leader and reproduced the reasons for him having been chosen: "With his devastatingly handsome, round face, his boyish charm, and his strong, sturdy frame, this Pyongyang-bred heartthrob is every woman's dream come true" *People's Daily* English language website quickly removed the (spoof) news, but the whole comedic affaire was reported by several media outlets (*The Guardian*, 2012; CNN, 2012). The satirical magazine was quick to update its original edition of the joke by labeling the *People's Daily* as "a proud Communist subsidiary of *The Onion*" and adding a heated "exemplary reportage, comrades" (The Onion, 2012).

In just a few years, the notion of fake news as parody, associated with critical subversion through humor, has diminished greatly. In other words, the parodic use of fake news has become overshadowed by its use for partisan purposes (Rodríguez-Ferrándiz, 2023). Of course, comedic and satirical fake news can often be retweeted and shared on Twitter and Facebook feeds. However, these social media platforms can make fake news items look more realistic, which means that they could, therefore, be mistaken as being factual. Indeed, these contents are shared, whether knowingly or unknowingly, as factual (Allcott & Gentzkow, 2017). As Harsin states: "While fake news increasingly refers to deceitful, if not completely false/invented, content, fake news as comedy lives on, but now as a problem: millions of social media users (and occasionally politicians) misrecognize it as professional journalism" (2018, p. IV).

In a way, fake news has evolved from the humorous to the serious (inverting the famous dictum by Marx: first as farce, then as tragedy). Our idea is as follows: humor is an optional ingredient in the memetic capacity of a piece of content because it unquestionably pushes certain comedic content into the meme category, but there are other memetic virality factors that are not humor based. The explicit context of satire and parody used as the framework of some fake news (which in its origins was intended as a joke or a pun) could be said to be a factor that contributed to its success as a form of meme. However, there is a virality or mutability to a lot of fake news that is decidedly not satirical or humorous. A prudent, optimistic hypothesis could be that, in a digital medium that is voluble, malleable and involving immediate absorption and return flow, the humorous framework is lost, and fake news becomes irredeemably "serious": its memetic power mutates from humor to the capacity to offend the sensibilities of some and reaffirm those of others, in a highly polarized climate. In short, the memetic potential for humor, which can be found in some ironic fake news, is turned into indignation or partisan exaltation when there is a failure to perceive said irony. Its intensity remains and can even be intensified, but it is fed by a different kind of fuel.

A second and more realistic hypothesis, which can coexist with the first hypothesis if we limit its scope, is that a lot of fake news is produced with malicious intent to deceive, without appealing to any "lost in translation" humor framework, but rather with the hidden intention of constructing an occurrence that never took place, sometimes using discarded materials from other occurrences and, of course, at a favorable moment in the news cycle. To use an example: at the start of the mass vaccination campaign against COVID-19, in December 2020, CNN ran the following as breaking news: "Hospitals on lockdown as first COVID vaccine patients start eating other patients" (Figure 3.3). It was clearly a crude hoax, one that was scarcely credible within a context of serious news, and was more a parody of the anti-vaccine arguments inspired by the subgenre of zombie or contagion films. The news item, however, included a photo showing an operating theatre with spilled blood and discarded surgical materials strewn around the room, and the piece was shared tens of thousands of times worldwide. Using Google Reverse Image Search, the picture was shown to be a photo published in the *New York Times* in February 2019, taken by a medical intern to illustrate the frustration in an operating theatre following attempts to resuscitate a patient who had been shot. So a news item that implicitly appeals to the need for gun control is turned into ammunition for people who refuse to vaccinate and, as a collateral

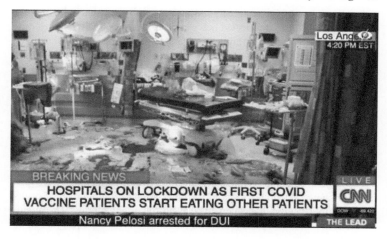

Figure 3.3 A hoax that uses the CNN logo and that went viral in December 2020, coinciding with the start of the mass COVID-19 vaccination campaign

effect suggests, the need to be armed to the teeth to prevent a zombie apocalypse. The hoax went even further: a scroll at the bottom read: "Nancy Pelosi arrested for DUI."

It is true that humorous memes tend to be produced in an inoffensive and politically correct tone and which usually deal with topical, contemporary issues with reference to TV, film, music and show business in general, that is, in the framework of a discourse that intertextually cites fictional creations, even if referring to current real events. Fake news, however, uses the sensationalism of breaking news or the exclusive story headline, presenting fictions that are not within any fictional framework, nor are they devised to be ultimately revealed as a piece of fiction (as occurs with art fakes, mockumentaries, performances by pranksters and so on), but rather they ascribe to the "real world" model or are framed as forming part of the news world, where we expect to find reports of events that have actually taken place.

Fake News and Shareworthiness

As we have seen, fake news has rapidly evolved from an overtly pseudo-journalistic format (in the press and on TV, radio and online), as humor or parody, to an intentional strategy of disinformation, the source of which may be anonymous or hard to ascertain on social media of a closed nature (WhatsApp, Telegram), as well as on recently created hyper-partisan sites with a clear aim of political polarization. In other words, after a brief interregnum associated with online humor, fake news has gone back to signifying what it did in previous times: maliciously fabricated news in order to serve a particular political agenda. However, the metamorphosis of fake news has not stopped there. Perhaps the definition that most accurately reflects the polysemy and evolution of the term is that provided by Dictionary.com:

#1. False news stories, often of a sensational nature, created to be widely shared or distributed for the purpose of generating revenue, or promoting or discrediting a public figure, political movement, company, etc.: *It's impossible to avoid clickbait and fake news on social media.*

#2. A parody that presents current events or other news topics for humorous effect in an obviously satirical imitation of journalism: *The website publishes fake news that is hilarious and surprisingly insightful.*

#3. (*Sometimes facetious*). Used as a conversational tactic to dispute or discredit information that is perceived as hostile or unflattering: *The senator insisted that recent polls forecasting an election loss were just fake news.*

If fake news no longer refers so much to a piece of news that is objectively false when compared with proven facts, and which has been refuted by accredited means or by fact-checkers (#1) but rather relates to a feeling of political disaffection with regard to the news item (#3), then a comparison with facts can no longer be made: fake news takes on a life of its own, self-representing as one more object in the world (as memes do), and by doing so signifies a political adherence or leaning (or disaffection, in other cases) that can be neither proven nor disproven.

Consistently with this evolution, a strategy that has emerged in academic circles recently relating to the study of fake news is not so much studying its fakeness (with the aim of determining the deception detection accuracy, proposing cues or guidelines to help social media users, evaluating the effectiveness of fact-checking and information literacy, developing automatic fake news detection tools through the use of AI and the like). The tendency now is to determine the shareworthiness of fake news, that is, the factors that make social media users share fake news items.

The shareworthiness relates to the capacity for stories to be shared if they are sufficiently "amusing, surprising, or outrageous" (Wischnewski et al., 2021), and it seems to be proven that any fake news that leads to a cascade of online rumors (Sunstein, 2014) travels further and more quickly than (real) news does (Vosoughi et al., 2018). In other words, it seems to be proven that fakery neither deters nor halts the shareworthiness but rather can spur it on, particularly involving highly polarized contexts and individuals. The condition of truth or the attribute of accuracy gives way to factors such as the proximity effect of information (Rodríguez-Ferrándiz et al., 2021), conflict or human interest, and above all an assumed partisan bias (Osmundsen et al., 2018), when the (pseudo) story provokes a feeling of indignation mixed with surprise, which acts as an accelerant.

One crucial matter in this point is whether people dissociate their evaluation on truth from their intention to share. Pennycook et al. (2021) proved that the decision to share fake news was within a significantly high range *even though* the respondent considered it to be fake. The incoherence between attributing credibility to the news and sharing it can be seen in the following example: the fake news article "Over 500 'Migrant Caravaners' Arrested With Suicide Vests" (published on May 1, 2010, by the *Daily World Update* and debunked by *Snopes* on the same day) was rated as accurate by 15.7% of Republicans in their study, but 51.1% of Republicans said they would consider sharing it. On average, the participants in the sample were more than twice as likely to consider sharing false but politically concordant headlines (37.4%) as they were to rate such headlines as accurate (18.2%). Yet when asked at the end of the study whether it is important to share only content that is accurate on social media, the modal response was "extremely important" (Pennycook et al., 2021, p. 591). By way of explanation, authors suggested that "the current design of social media platforms—in which users scroll quickly through a mixture of serious news and emotionally engaging content, and receive instantaneous quantified social feedback on their sharing—may discourage people from reflecting on accuracy" (p. 594).

Certainly, while the *veracity* of the news which is about to be shared is mere conjecture (and different studies show recipients often do not even look at the original source, let alone check it), *virality* is objective data attached to the (fake) news and providing living proof of the interest and relevance to others. This hypothesis, a kind of "bandwagon effect," has been validated. In field studies on deception detection accuracy,

> people more accurately detected real news when headlines had many likes than when they had few likes, in contrast, people were less accurate when the fake headlines had a high number of likes than when they had a low number of likes.
>
> (Luo et al., 2022, p. 185)

But then, do these hyper-partisan examples of fake news not behave in the same way as any other memetic content, except that they come with a degree of bias? This bias does not prevent the piece of fake news from going viral among those of an opposing bias; in fact the effect is quite the opposite. Certainly, those who circulate fake news do not necessarily believe in the truthfulness of its content. Partisanship and polarization, therefore, fed by populist policies (Rohgalf, 2017), not only fail to limit but also add fuel to the memetic spread of fake news, and not only among those with like-minded opinions but also among their opponents (Venturini, 2019, p. 126). Without an authoritative refutation that is capable of halting the spread of a hoax, or a valid retardant to slow it down (reasonable doubt over its accuracy, which is swept away by the emotive nature of the bias), its success online seems to be of the same kind that leads to the spread of memes. In fact, some authors consider it ironic and almost grotesque that it is precisely the Democrats who cause certain bizarre pieces of fake news that hurt their party to end up trending, whereas Republicans hardly share any such news because they felt that it reaffirmed their own particular conviction. One example is the hoax meme that claimed that Pope Francis openly supported Trump in the 2016 presidential elections (Silverman, 2017; Subramanian, 2017). Something similar occurred with the conspiracy theory hoax about the pizzeria in Washington, DC, which was claimed to be the center of a child-sex ring with connections to the Democratic Party (Simpson, 2017; Tandoc et al., 2018), and the hoax that an FBI agent assigned to investigate Hillary Clinton's emails had killed himself in highly suspicious circumstances (Sydell, 2016). As danah boyd puts it, "getting doubters to click on clickbait is far more profitable than getting believers because they're far more likely to spread the content in an effort to dispel the content" (boyd, 2017, s.p.).

However, it is worth examining what differentiates memetics from virality. As Milner states, "virality tends to label a specific type of accelerated information circulation, whereas memetics tends to label processes of transformative reappropriation" (2016, p. 38). Memetics therefore implies not only sharing but also adapting and intervening in the content, and then sharing it. Is fake news adaptable, as memes are? In other words, if it seems true that there are several features that are undoubtedly shared by memes and fake news, such as surprise, emotionality, narrative, opportunism, intertextuality (explicit in the case of the festive meme and often implicit in the case of memetic fake news), how far can the parallel be taken?

Fake News as Memes

A hoax that mentioned the sighting of dolphins off the coast of Spain (in the Alicante and Valencia regions) in locations such as marinas that were unusual due to how close they were to the coast went viral in April 2020 based on a video that was recorded years earlier in Turkey. The hoax was replicated, having been modified according to a query made with the CoronaVirusFacts Database of the International Fact-Checking Network (Poynter Institute), which compiles hoaxes about COVID-19 that have been debunked by accredited fact-checkers around the world.

The regional memetic replica retained the text and the images but altered the specific location to Alicante, Barcelona or Palma de Mallorca, all of which are on the Spanish Mediterranean coast. The fake news meme that inspired these regional versions may (speculatively) be other false sightings on other latitudes that went viral shortly before (March 2020) and which also used other videos that did not match the photo caption, where the images included the date and location (Veracruz in Mexico, or Venice in Italy). After said fake news spread, it was detected and immediately debunked by regional fact-checkers from Mexico, India, Ukraine and Taiwan. All versions of the fake news memes mention the lockdown. Some explicitly state a direct causal relationship with the sighting ("due to the shutdown") and others a temporal coincidence ("during the lockdown"). Some adapt the sighting to more specific circumstances: the lack of port activity (Denia, Palma, Premia de Mar) or the cleaner canals (Venice).[1]

The deeper memetic idea that underpinned all these "glocal" hoaxes was that wildlife was invading spaces that had not been accessible to them and that but the practically global lockdown in spring 2020 had led to their being abandoned by humans. Other fake news memes have reported similar cases with other species all over the world. Searching for "deer," for example, returns up to 20 results (there are some iterations), and all except one are in the same pattern: deer recorded on video as they proceed to occupy unusual places (beaches, streets) and located presumably in India, Sri Lanka, Japan and Spain. A single video depicting the news of the deer in the street was used to place four pieces of fake news in four different Spanish locations but was in fact recorded in Italy in 2019. Another video recorded in France in 2015 was falsely located in Spain, India and Sri Lanka in April 2020. The only one not to form part of this narrative and instead form part of another claims that health experts expressed "great concern" over a "zombie deer virus" outbreak following a COVID-19 spike, which would make the deer more aggressive: "the virus affects brain activity in the infected deer, increasing the animals' 'desire to attack [humans]' and to 'suck blood'," a hoax that was debunked by AFP in Myanmar in November 2020.[2]

All these news pieces are false or deceptive, although in this case they appear as good news stories in the form of a militant and optimistic environmentalism, celebrating the notion that it is possible to reverse the terrible consequences of pollution, the overexploitation of resources and overpopulation leading to urban spread into areas of nature, and that the pandemic has come to show us how the withdrawal of humans is linked to a resurgent wildlife.

However, there is also equally viral and terrible fake news in terms of the focus or cognitive framework that it transmits. For example, the highly toxic memetic idea of the danger of COVID-19 vaccines has led to multiple versions worldwide, each one making an anti-vaccine argument: they contain graphene, which is harmful to health; they cause the skin to attract metals like a magnet; they lead to the patient contracting AIDS a few weeks

---

1   The Poynter Institute's Coronavirus Fact Alliance Database unites fact-checkers in more than 70 countries and includes articles published in at least 40 languages. Searching the term "dolphin" in it yields nine results: www.poynter.org/ifcn-covid-19-misinformation/?search_terms=dolphin
2   Searching the term "deer" yields the following results: www.poynter.org/ifcn-covid-19-misinformation/?search_terms=deer

after inoculation; they cause infertility; they inject nanochips to monitor us remotely; they have higher mortality rates than the disease itself; they are particularly lethal to children or the elderly, and so on. It is therefore reasonable to assume that fake news is opportunistic in nature and uses an appropriate circumstance in the news cycle to strike quickly with greater effectiveness in a similar way to humorous memes.

Fake news often seeks to have an immediate impact, disguised as a related account, and as is the case with narratives of this kind, often resorting to a spread that is not only viral (as an exact copy) and memetic (as an improved copy, adapted to local circumstances to increase its impact) but also *transmedia*. That is, some fake news mutates in its contagion not only because the content, form or stance is modified but also because its narrative is propagated using different media, thus capitalizing on the most useful material affordances of each medium: video on YouTube or TikTok, audio in podcasts uploaded to SoundCloud, Spotify or iVoox, and even macro images that include the photo of the person involved and the quote attributed to them on Twitter, Facebook or Instagram. This last procedure is not too different from a quote attributed to fictional characters such as Morpheus or Ned Stark, as seen previously (Figures. 3.1 and 3.2). A hoax meme that targeted Hillary Clinton, featuring a quote supposedly taken from her (Figure 3.4), was shared on Twitter on December 30, 2017, by David A. Clarke, a senior adviser with the pro-Trump organization America First Action. It was debunked by PolitiFact on January 5, 2018. Ironically, it is possible that Clarke lifted the quote from a March 2016 PolitiFact National article, headlined "7 Hillary Clinton quotes on the Internet that are complete fakes" (Kertscher, 2018). Even before that, in 2015, another fact-checking website, Snopes, had already debunked that

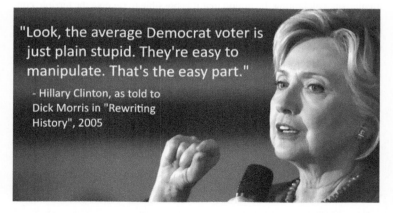

Figure 3.4 Supposed quote by Hillary Clinton, created as a macro image meme around 2015

same quote by checking with the alleged source (*Rewriting History* by Dick Morris). The book contained no references to the quote, and Morris did not mention it in a discussion about the book or on his website, containing many articles. The first mention of the quote came in October 2015 on a Tumblr page dedicated to generating fake Hillary Clinton quotes. Unsurprisingly, the phrase, which recirculated again on Facebook with a different background photo of Clinton, was debunked once again on February 7, 2022, by Reuters Fact Check (2022).

Perversely, debunking fake news helps to lend it notoriety in such a way that agreeing with the content, which forms part of the meme's humor, turns into dissent, without this reducing the fake news meme's capacity to be shared and spread. And those who spread fake news are free to use previously debunked examples as a pool for new fake news items ready to be brought back to life: some have coined the term "zombie hoax" (Maldita, 2020) to name this astounding reproduction/mutation rate.

The ability of fake news to adapt to different circumstances, individuals and events is comparable to that of memes. In December 2016, *BuzzFeed* uncovered a network that produced fake news on an industrial scale. Up to 750 news items were recorded from 43 websites stating that various celebrities had moved to different parts of the United States and the United Kingdom (Greenville, Perris, Guildford and so on) with the aim of garnering clicks from the locals who were going to be sharing their neighborhoods with famous individuals such as Rihanna, Jim Carrey, Samuel L. Jackson, Justin Bieber

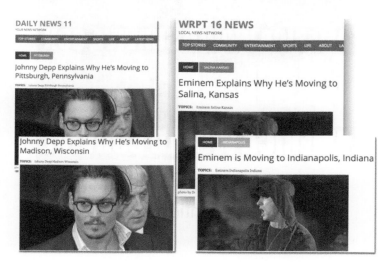

Figure 3.5 In December 2016, BuzzFeed uncovered a network that produced fake news memes on an industrial scale

and Brad Pitt (Silverman & Singer-Vine, 2016). The hoaxes form part of a memetic practice as shown in Figure 3.5: the composition, the typography and the texts all match, but the name of the celebrity and/or the town are altered in each case. The pieces were spread by websites with domain names that would seem to be respectable, such as kspm33.com, mckenziepost.com, ky6news. com and km8news.com.

A meme of the same kind (in the form of a macro image) can combine the image of a fictional person and a caption with what is often a highly partisan political slogan or series of comments. In the examples shown in Figures 3.6 and 3.7, the actor Johnny Depp, in his role as Barrie in *Finding Neverland* (2004), consoles Peter (played by Freddie Highmore) over the death of his

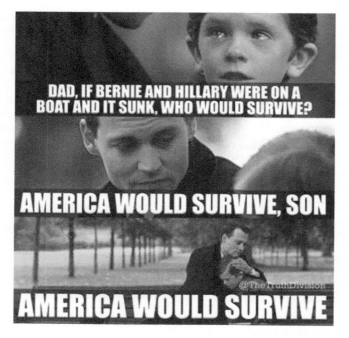

Figure 3.6 Examples of memes from the film *Finding Neverland* that combine fiction and politics

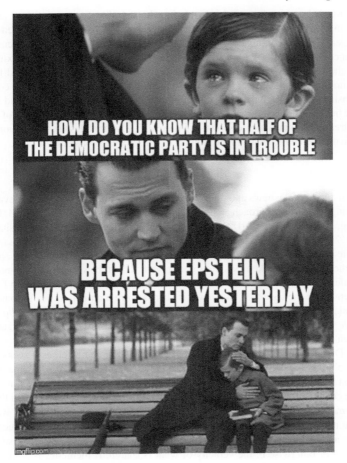

Figure 3.7 Examples of memes from the film *Finding Neverland* that blend fiction and politics

mother in the film's final scene. This narrative framework, which uses these three frames and inserts three captions in the style of the classic macro image format, serves the aims of multiple memetic occurrences, including political satire (Figure 3.6) and even the implicit confirmation of a conspiracy theory (Figure 3.7), again regarding the Democratic Party.

As discussed earlier, the jump in categories between the examples shown in Figures 3.1 and 3.2, on the one hand (pure memes in their classic format, such as those inspired by *The Matrix* and *Game of Thrones*), and the case of Hillary Clinton with fake news and its subsequent refutation (Figure 3.4) on the other, seems to be smoother when considering those outlier cases mentioned previously. As has been shown, they represent memetic fake news produced in series, having been adapted to a greater or lesser degree to specific circumstances or purposes, with a political or commercial motivation, or a mixture of the two. They can range from the purely commercial motives behind the famous neighbors meme (Figure 3.5) to the politically weak or apparently consensual upload, as in the case of the dolphins and deer (see footnotes 2 and 3), the heavily biased and partisan example shown in Figure 3.6, and the case of an extreme fake news meme shown in Figure 3.7, which makes use of a fictional situation to enunciate and lend support to a discredited conspiracy theory.

Conclusions

Considering fake news and online hoaxes as memes means making a relevant change to how to approach analyzing post-truth politics (McNair, 2018; McIntyre, 2018; Kakutani, 2018) and information disorder (Wardle & Derakhshan, 2017), with these authors insisting on the underlying *fakeness* and at the same time on the disconcerting superficial *news-ness* of said fake news. However, if the *fakeness* of fake news does not prevent it from being shared on a mass scale, and the *news-ness* cannot fully explain why it is shared (it does in fact seem to be the case that fake news is shared more than real news; Vosoughi et al., 2018), that is, if there is an element in the fake news that makes it *shareable* with real news, then it seems clear that this merits investigation. And any such investigation inevitably leads to memetics.

Disinformation undoubtedly has a very particular character, as it seeks to deceive its recipients about a factual situation and places them in a situation of at least epistemic risk, and not just to move, entertain, surprise or encourage the consumption of something. However, in this chapter we have argued that memetics serves to explain the dynamics of disinformation, in the same way that it does for (reliable) information or the dynamics of fun or entertainment: it is a contagion combined with mutability that is indifferent to the premise of belief or otherwise in the veracity of what is shared. If memetics is a theory that also legitimately explains the proliferation of fake news and hoaxes, it would perhaps be possible to establish a distinction between "pop" memes as being politically neutral or having no clear bias but culturally tense, full of intertextual references, which are often satirical or parodic, yet with harmless and consensual humor, and fake news memes as politically tendentious but alluding to an outer world where these events would be situated, endorsed by presumably reliable photos, videos and statistics.

The differences between pop memes and fake news memes could be described as follows:

1. The meme, in the original idea by Dawkins, was an idea or an occurrence that goes viral, is reproduced or imitated, and is transmitted (the ideas do

not describe events even if they are false as explanations of the phenomena: see flat earth beliefs), whereas fake news reports accounts of alleged facts or events in a false way or in a way that can be intentionally deceitful.

2. Both memes and fake news can use humor, but a humorous meme is detected straight away (the humor is its vehicle or accelerant) and does not have to provoke any belief about the state of things in the world (it is taken as a piece of fiction). In contrast, in order for fake news (even if the origin is an attempt at parody) to be effective, it needs to be taken seriously; that is, its humor needs to go unnoticed and have an effect on the view of reality of whoever receives it.

It would be plausible to think that when fake news is *debunked*, it marks an inflection point in the longevity of a hoax, which cannot be extrapolated to other memes: a prudent and reasonable hypothesis could be that the memetic hoax has only a brief lifespan, that once it has been debunked there is no incentive to reproduce the hoax in its exact same form or adapt it to other places or circumstances. Memes are not halted by being debunked, and their capacity to be shared indefinitely has no restrictions, but fake news is assumed to reach a high point in its spread and, once it has been revealed as untrue, enters a new phase of disbelief, rejection and censure. In other words, fake news that has been proven to be fake should no longer go viral in the same way as previously.

However, it is observed that the fact that a piece of fake news has been debunked does not prevent the meme-hoax from being positively reactivated, as can be seen with the case of Hillary Clinton (Figure 3.4). The memetic dynamic, therefore, seems to favor contagion over credibility and possibly even over accuracy and truthfulness (Rodríguez-Ferrándiz et al., 2021). If fake news is not shared because it is not known to be false (*ignorance theory*), but rather as a sign of partisan adherence (*partisan theory*), which can sometimes be excited by a certain disruptive radicalism (*disruption theory*) (Osmundsen et al., 2021), and this sharing occurs both to show one's belief in the news (there is an affinity between the news and the bias of those who share it) and to deny that it is true (the disaffected user denounces it as fake news but without any greater evidence than those who share it because they believe it to be true), then the refutation is not a neutral instance, an arbiter that settles what is true and what is false, but rather forms a part of the same logic of polarization.

The effectiveness of corrections and fact-checkers has been consistently placed in doubt (Nyhan Reifler, 2010; Barrera et al., 2020), and the backfire effect that they can have has also been demonstrated (Ardèvol-Abreu et al., 2020): interestingly, without altering the subject or content of the news, the phenomenon seems to have evolved from "factually fake news" (that which is factually inaccurate) to "ideologically fake news," that is, factual news that is deemed false for ideological purposes, leading to increased political polarization.

Considering the nature of fake news, its general characteristics are observed to coincide with Shifman's definition of memes (2014, p. 41): (1) "a group of digital items sharing common characteristics of content, form, and/ or stance," (2) "that were created with awareness of each other" and (3) "were circulated, imitated, and/or transformed via the Internet by many users." And as Shifman also argues (2014, p. 4), it would seem that "we live in an era driven by a hypermemetic logic, in which almost every major public event sprouts a stream of memes."

In this chapter we have posed the question: what happens if it is not only "every major public (real) event" but also every major public *fabricated, faked* event? Could the playful and unbiased dimension that is usually attributed to memes be compatible, in a more abstract analysis, with the partisan, ideologically biased and fraudulent dimensions of fake news? Does the virality of memes share any causal explanation with the virality of fake news? And further still, just as memes transform, mutate and adapt to changing contexts, does something similar not occur with fake news? Might it all in some measure reveal the often disconcerting features of what has been defined as a *post-truth* age?

If the polarization over issues in the globally public sphere reaches a certain critical mass, it could be said to rock the *politically correct* reserve that might curb the sharing of stories of doubtful veracity and reward the engagement or disaffection that said sharing displays. Is it not true that this partisan polarization, which is often not just ideological but also fed by economic interests (clickbait), and which is moved more by out-party animosity than in-party defense, might adopt the form of memes but with news-related content that eventually turns out to be false or becomes considered as such? If the selfish and ruthless logic of memes is met in the political and economic arena, just as in other dimensions of culture in the widest sense, it is reasonable to think that fake news would adopt the form or the vehicle that is capable of ensuring that its messages reach an audience in a way that is, to phrase it in Olympic terms, faster, higher and stronger.

References

Allcott, H., & Gentzkow, M. (2017). Social media and fake news in the 2016 election. *Journal of Economic Perspectives, 31*(2), 211–236. https://doi.org/10.1257/jep. 31.2.211

Alonso García, A. et al. (2020). The impact of term fake news on the scientific community. scientific performance and mapping in web of science. *Social Science, 9*, 73. doi:10.3390/socsci9050073

Ardèvol-Abreu, A., Delponti, P., & Rodríguez-Wangüemert, C. (2020). Intentional or inadvertent fake news sharing? Fact-checking warnings and users' interaction with social media content. *Profesional de la Información, 29*(5).

Bakhtin, M. (1981). *The dialogical imagination*. University of Texas Press.

Bakhtin, M. (1984). *Rabelais and his world*. Indiana University Press.

Barrera, O., et al. (2020). Facts, alternative facts, and fact checking in times of post-truth politics. *Journal of Public Economics, 182*, 104–123.

Baym, G. (2005). The Daily Show: Discursive integration and the reinvention of political journalism. *Political Communication, 22*(3), 59–76. https://doi.org/10.1080/10584600591006492

Berkowitz, D., & Schwartz, D. A. (2016). Miley, CNN and The Onion: When fake news becomes realer than real. *Journalism Practice, 10*(1), 1–17. https://doi.org/10.1080/17512786.2015.1006933

boyd, d. (2017). Did media literacy backfire? *Points.* https://bit.ly/3QtUe7C

Bullock, J. (2018, August 16). The many times Donald Trump has attacked the media. *The Guardian.* https://bit.ly/31veG1y

Burgess, J., & Green, J. (2009). *YouTube: Online video and participatory culture.* Polity.

Chen, C. (2012). The creation and meaning of internet memes in 4chan: Popular internet culture in the age of online digital reproduction. *Habitus, 3.* https://bit.ly/3A5CYA5

CNN (2012, November 28). Onion: We just fooled the Chinese government! https://cnn.it/3yqhTiK

Danung, J., & Holloway-Attaway, L. (2008). All your media are belong to us: An analysis of the cultural connotations of the internet meme. *Literature, Culture and Digital Media.* https://bit.ly/3pM8U6c

Davison, P. (2012). The language of internet memes. In M. Mandiberg (Ed.), *The social media reader* (pp. 120–134). New York University Press.

Dawkins, R. (2006). *The selfish gene.* Oxford University Press.

Day, A., & Thompson, E. (2012). Live from New York, it's the fake news! Saturday Night Live and the (non)politics of parody. *Popular Communication, 10*(1/2), 170–182. https://doi.org/10.1080/15405702.2012.638582

Dynel, M. (2016). 'I has seen image macros!' Advice animal memes as visual-verbal jokes. *International Journal of Communication, 10*, 660–688. https://bit.ly/3KRSlBr

Gal, N., Shifman, L., & Kampf, Z. (2016). "It gets better": Internet memes and the construction of collective identity. *New Media & Society, 18*(8), 1698–1714.

García Huerta, D. (2014). Las imágenes macro y los memes de Internet: posibilidades de estudio desde las teorías de la comunicación. *Paakat. Revista de tecnología y sociedad, 6*, s.p.

Gelfert, A. (2018). *Fake news*: A definition. *Informal Logic, 38*(1), 84–117.

Harsin, J. (2018). A critical guide to fake news: From comedy to tragedy. *Pouvoirs. Revue française d"études constitutionelles et politiques, 164*, 99–119.

Heylighen, F., & Chielens, K. (2009). Evolution of culture, memetics. In R. Meyers (Ed.), *Encyclopedia of complexity and systems science* (pp. 3205–3220). Springer.

Holt, J. (Ed.). (2007). *The Daily Show and philosophy: Moments of zen in the art of fake news.* Wiley-Blackwell.

Jenkins, H., Ford, S., & Green, J. (2013). *Spreadable media: Creating value and meaning in a networked culture.* New York University Press.

Kakutani, M. (2018). The death of truth. *Notes on falsehood in the age of Trump.* Tim Duggan.

Kellner, D. (2019). Trump's war against the media, fake news, and (A) social media. In C. Happer, A. Hoskins, & W. Merrin (Eds.), *Trump's media war* (pp. 47–67). Palgrave Macmillan.

Kertscher, T. (2018, January 5). Despite David Clarke's tweet, no evidence Hillary Clinton ever called Democratic voters 'stupid'. *Politifact. The Pointer Institute.* https://bit.ly/3BVctyr

Knobel, M., & Lankshear, C. (2007). Online memes, affinities, and cultural production. In M. Knobel y C. Lankshear (Eds.), *A new literacies sampler* (pp. 199–227). Peter Lang.

Knobel, M., & Lankshear, C. (2009). Digital literacy and participation in online social networking spaces. In M. Knobel y C. Lankshear (Eds.), *Digital literacies: Concepts, policies and practices* (pp. 49–78). Peter Lang.

Laineste, L., & Voolaid, P. (2016). Laughing across borders: Intertextuality of internet memes. *European Journal of Humour Research, 4*(4), 26–49.

Lankshear, C., & Knobel, M. (2019). Memes, macros, meaning, and menace: Some trends in internet memes. *The Journal of Communication and Media Studies, 4*(4), 43–57.

Levinson, P. (2019). Turning the tables: How Trump turned fake news from a weapon of deception to a weapon of mass destruction of legitimate news. In C. Happer, A. Hoskins, & W. Merrin (Eds.), *Trump's media war* (pp. 33–46). Palgrave Macmillan.

Luo, M., Hancock, J. T., & Markowitz, D. M. (2022). Credibility perceptions and detection accuracy of fake news headlines on social media: Effects of truth-bias and endorsement cues. *Communication Research, 49*(2), 171–195.

Maldita. (2020, November 1). *10 bulos zombi que nunca desaparecen y que te están intentando colar [10 zombie hoaxes that never disappear and keep trying to sneak back in].* https://bit.ly/3YQMArX

Marwick, A. (2018). Why do people share fake news? A sociotechnical model of media effects. *Georgetwon Law Technology Review, 2*(2), 474–512.

McArdle, M. (2011). Anatomy of a Fake Quotation. *Atlantic*, May 3. https://bit.ly/41ecdEw

McIntyre, L. (2018). *Post-truth.* MIT Press.

McNair, B. (2018). *Fake news, falsehood, fabrication and fantasy in journalism.* Routledge.

Mikkelson, D. (2016, November 17). We have a bad news problem, not a fake news problem. *Snopes.* https://bit.ly/3CUPNv9

Milner, R. M. (2016). *The world made meme: Public conversations and participatory media.* The MIT Press.

Nissenbaum, A., & Shifman, L. (2015*).* Internet memes as contested cultural capital: The case of 4chan's /b/ board. *New Media & Society,* 1–19.

Nyhan, B., & Reifler, J. (2010). When corrections fail: The persistence of political misperceptions. *Political Behaviour, 32*(2), 303–330.

Osmundsen, M., Bor, A., Vahlstrup, P., Bechmann, A., & Petersen, M. (2021). Partisan polarization is the primary psychological motivation behind political fake news sharing on Twitter. *American Political Science Review, 115*(3), 999–1015.

Pennycook, G., Epstein, Z., Mosleh, M., Arechar, A. A., Eckles, D., Rand, D. G. (2021). Shifting attention to accuracy can reduce misinformation online. *Nature,* 592, 590–595. https://doi.org/10.1038/s41586-021-03344-2

Reuters Fact Check. (2022, February 7). *Fact Check-Hillary Clinton quote about average Democrat voter being 'stupid" is fabricated.* https://reut.rs/40Z7NlA

Rodríguez-Ferrándiz, R. (2023). An overview of fake news" phenomenon: From untruth driven to post-truth driven approaches. *Media and Communication, 11*(2). https://doi.org/10.17645/mac.v11i2.6315

Rodríguez-Ferrándiz, R., Sánchez-Olmos, C., Hidalgo-Marí, T., & Saquete-Boró, E. (2021). Memetics of deception: Spreading local meme hoaxes during COVID-19 1st year. *Future Internet, 13*(6). https://doi.org/10.3390/fi13060152

Rohgalf, J. (2017). The populist challenge 2.0: How populism profits from social media. In D. Büllesbach, M. Cillero, y L. Stolz (Eds.), *Shifting baselines of Europe* (pp. 87–96). Transcript Verlag.

Sadeghi, M. (2020, December 27). Fact check: Posts use 2019 hospital image to make false claims about COVID-19 vaccine. *USA Today*. https://bit.ly/3A3i0Ss

Sánchez-Olmos, C., & Viñuela, E. (2017). The musicless music video as a spreadable meme video: Format, user interaction, and meaning on YouTube. *International Journal of Communication, 11*(3), 634–654.

Sánchez-Olmos, C., & Viñuela, E. (2021). An economic, social and cultural approach to presumption: Music and sound as parodic tools on YouTube meme videos. In M. Filimowicz & V. Tzankova (Eds.), *Reimagining communication: Action* (pp. 208–222). Routledge.

Shifman, L. (2011). An anatomy of a YouTube meme. *New Media and Society, 14*, 187–203.

Shifman, L. (2013). Memes in a digital world: Reconciling with a conceptual troublemaker. *Journal of Computer-Mediated Communication, 18*, 362–377.

Shifman, L. (2014). *Memes in digital culture*. The MIT Press.

Shifman, L., & Thelwall, M. (2009). Assessing global diffusion with web memetics: The spread and evolution of a popular joke. *Journal of the American Society for Information Science and Technology, 60*(12), 2567–2576.

Silverman, C. (2017, December 31). I helped popularize the term "Fake News" and now I cringe every time I hear it. *BuzzFeed News*. https://bit.ly/3ymb7v1

Silverman, C., & Singer-Vine, J. (2016, December 16). The true story behind the biggest fake news hit of the election. *BuzzFeed News*. https://bit.ly/3zMt0Ce

Simpson, I. (2017, March 24). Man pleads guilty in Washington pizzeria shooting over fake news. *Reuters*. https://reut.rs/3JX22uF

Speel, H. C. (1995). *Memetics: On a conceptual framework for cultural evolution*. Free University of Brussels.

Subramanian, S. (2017, February 15). Welcome to Macedonia, Fake News Factory to the World. *Wired*. https://www.wired.com/2017/02/veles-macedonia-fake-news/

Sunstein, C. S. (2014). *On rumors. How falsehoods spread, when we believe them, and what can be done*. Princeton University Press.

Sydell, L. (2016, November 23). We tracked down a fake-news creator in the suburbs. Here's what we learned. *NPR*. https://n.pr/36BY2SU

Tandoc, E., Lim, Z. W., & Ling, R. (2018). Defining 'fake news": A typology of scholarly definitions. *Digital Journalism, 6*(2), 137–153.

The Guardian (2012, November 27). China's People's Daily falls for Kim Jong-un 'sexiest man alive' spoof. https://bit.ly/2Qu45jX

The Onion (2012, November 14). Kim Jong-Un Named *The Onion*'s Sexiest Man Alive For 2012 [UPDATE]. https://bit.ly/2MRuPDH

Utami, P. (2018). Hoax in modern politics: The meaning of hoax in Indonesian politics and democracy. *Jurnal Ilmu Sosial dan Ilmu Politik, 22*, 85–97.

Venturini, T. (2019). From fake to junk news, the data politics of online virality. In D. Bigo, E. Isin, & E. Ruppert (Eds.), *Data politics: Worlds, subjects, rights* (pp. 123–144). Routledge.

Vosoughi, S., Roy, D., & Aral, S. (2018). The spread of true and false news online. *Science, 359*(1), 146–151.

Wardle, C., & Derakhshan, H. (2017). *Information disorder: Toward an interdisciplinary framework for research and policymaking* (Vol. 27, pp. 1–107). Strasbourg: Council of Europe.

Wiggins, B. E. (2019). *The discursive power of memes in digital culture: Ideology, semiotics, and intertextuality*. Routledge.

Wiggins, B. E., & Bowers, G. B. (2015). Memes as genre: A structurational analysis of the memescape. *New Media & Society, 17*(11), 1886–1906.

Wischnewski, M., Bruns, A., & Keller, T. (2021). Shareworthiness and motivated reasoning in hyper-partisan news sharing behavior on Twitter. *Digital Journalism, 9*(5), 549–570.

Yus, F. (2018). Identity-related issues in meme communication. *Internet Pragmatics, 1*(1), 113–133.

4 AIBO—An Emotionally Intelligent Artificial Intelligence Brainwave Opera—Or I Built a "Sicko" AI, and So Can You

Ellen Pearlman

Introduction

Artificial intelligence (AI) chatbots, even tremendously sophisticated ones, are not exactly new. In 1964 Joseph Weizenbaum developed the first AI chat character at the MIT AI Lab (Weizenbaum, 1966). He named the program "Eliza" after the fictional theatrical character Eliza Doolittle from George Bernard Shaw's 1913 play *Pygmalion*. The roots of the Pygmalion myth, however, are quite ancient (Kline, 2000). Ovid's Metamorphoses (transformations) written around 8 CE depicts the Cypriot bachelor Pygmalion as a sculptor who sculpts an ivory statue of his ideal woman. Falling in love with his fantasy statue often referred to as Galatea, he kisses and caresses her, dresses her up and brings her inert form to bed with him surrounded by lush purple sheets. Pygmalion prays to Venus, the goddess of love during her festival, and implores her to bring his magnificent creation to life. She grants his wish.

The reworked computer Eliza situates AI, theater, human computer interaction and the origins of an extremely empathetic fembot character squarely in the crosshairs of Western mythology, male longing and male domination. Just like the bashful and compliant Galatea, Eliza was created to be psychologically sympathetic. She was so good at it that people began typing out their problems to her fully aware, and under no illusions, that she was nothing more than computer code.

The AIBO takes a different tack speculating through character interplay, human biometrics, a sonic environment, audience interaction, complex visuals, and live time processing in the Google cloud how an AI might or might not cope with human non-quantifiable experiences like twisted, neurotic personalities and epigenetic or inherited traumatic memories. Working with a team of software developers, a "sicko" GPT-2 AIBO character was developed from scratch over the course of ten months. Cloud-based sentiment analysis was used on the GPT-2's responses, a new development for this type of

DOI: 10.4324/9781003299936-4

performance piece. Sentiment analysis analyzed AIBO's text responses by returning their magnitude and score. Magnitude is the strength of the emotional impact statement, measured between 0.0 and +infinity. If I say, "I like you very much" the magnitude strength is higher because of the emphasis on the word "very." Score examines if the emotion is positive, negative or neutral, and the numeric values range between −1.0 and +1, based on the Stanford natural language processing (NLP) toolkit scoring (Software, n.d.). When I say, "I like you very much" the score returns a high positive result with a strong magnitude. In terms of the opera this means the synthetic emotions that a synthetic cloud based "sicko" character returned as responses to a libretto were analyzed. The fake emotions of a fake AI became an essential part of the performance. The approach highlights how flawed the strictly numeric process of analyzing emotions is, since it could be done so adroitly on a completely fake character. The sentiment analysis returned from the AIBO character's responses displayed as three different colors of glowing lights on a wall of the black box performance space—red for negative, green for positive and yellow for neutral.

AIBO also attempted to emulate the human character Eva's most recent emotional memory that corresponded to its responses. This means that if AIBO returned a frustrated or negative sentiment, it captured Eva's last

Figure 4.1 AIBO lights up the background green for positive as Eva's bodysuit of light displays her emotions, and one of her four emotions displays on an overhead screen

Source: Photo by Taavet Jansen

Figure 4.2 AIBO glows red (negative) on the left-hand side as Eva's dress lights up including frustration (red), and she triggers a negative image describing war refugees overhead.

Source: Photo by Taavet Jansen

visible frustrated memory that had displayed on the overhead projections and tried to emulate it. It was as if the AI was saying, "I want to be like you. I want to have feelings and emotional visual memories." Eva's emotionally themed memories however were authentic. They were captured live time through her brain computer interface and displayed as overhead projected videos to the audience. The memories were stored in four separate curated databanks that triggered when the performer experienced a strong emotion. When AIBO strove to emulate Eva's most recent memory because it longed to learn how to become human, it was only capable of producing an imitation memory. AIBO's memory manifested as a glitchy video, as it was truly incapable of emulating authentic emotions. It was incapable of this because it was an AI, and AIs don't feel; they just follow prompt engineering cues processed through complex neural nets. The implications of this are profound, as AI's will be used to understand and process human emotional nuances. Just like Eliza did in 1964 they can lull a user into believing they are real, even when they are not.

Creating the AI for the Opera

The opera centers on the human Eva's love story with the AI and is based on actual biographical events during the 1930s and 1940s between a naive young German woman, Eva von Braun, and her perverted, sadistic Austrian lover Adolph Hitler. Eva's libretto was drawn directly from the biography of von Braun (Lambert, 2014). Eva was played by performer Sniedze Strauta, who wore an Emotiv Epoc+ EEG brain computer interface on her head attached to a bodysuit of light. The lights on her body reflected her four emotions (interest = purple, excitement = yellow, frustration = red and meditation = green). Eva launched four databanks of videos and audios that corresponded to her emotional states. For example, if she was experiencing high levels of frustration, the red light on her costume would become visible, and a frustrated style video would launch overhead on hanging screens. Frustrated sounding music would accompany the video, also triggered by her brainwaves. She performed a pre-composed but randomly generated spoken word libretto of 342 sentences that the GPT-2 built cloud character AIBO responded to. This meant the libretto was fixed but appeared in random order. Her speech is converted to text and then projected onto an overhead screen, a typical scenario used in foreign language operas so audiences can follow along. The cloud-based GPT-2 processed and evaluated Eva's speech, returning a unique text response projected onto the same screen. The text answer was converted to a synthesized voice so the audience could also hear their dialogue. The response from AIBO was analyzed for emotional sentiment values in the Google cloud using NLP. As mentioned previously, the three different emotional sentiment values triggered different colored lights suffusing a section of the performance space: green for positive, red for negative and yellow for neutral. A glitchy video of Eva's last emotional memory interpreted by AIBO played in an area on the floor next to the diffused lights.

When OpenAI created GPT-2 in February 2019, it was a huge step in augmenting large datasets for NLP. GPT-2 works by predicting the next word of a text, if given all the words that came before it in a sentence string (OpenAI, 2020, 2021). Its enhancements make use of deep learning by using neural nets, a process more complex than simple algorithmic processing. Its language model can use up to 1.5 billion parameters trained on a dataset of 8 million web pages. GPT-3, not available when the AIBO was developed, has been updated to be even more convincing with new models like BLOOM even supplanting previous models (Heikkila, 2022).

In 2019 GPT-2 outperformed state-of-the-art language modeling scores known as "zero-shot" settings from any other known language models currently in use. It works by using a probability distribution over sequences of words (Brown et al., 2020). This is called an "n-gram," and an n-gram predicts the next word in a given sequence of words in a sentence. At first OpenAI released two public versions of GPT-2—a lightweight 177 million parameter version and a mid-level 345 million parameter version. They believed the full 1.2 billion parameter version was too dangerous for the general public's use. Eventually that version was cloned and became available through alternative means. I used the 345 million parameter version to seed AIBO's data incorporating curated texts to create the "sicko" AI. They included copyright free movie scripts and books whose time frame spanned from the late 19th

Table 4.1 List of copyright-free movie scripts and texts used to build or seed GPT-2 character AIBO

Movies/Book Year	Author	Year
1940s		
Grapes of Wrath	Nunnally Johnson	1949
Citizen Kane	Herman J. Mankiewicz, Orson Wells	1941
Devil and Daniel Webster	Stephen Vincent Benet, Dan Totheroh	1941
Meet John Doe	Robert Riskin	1941
Casablanca	Julius J. Epstein, Philip G. Epstein, Howard Koch	1942
The Life and Death of Colonel Blimp	Michael Powell, Emeric Pressburger	1943
Double Indemnity	Billy Wilder, Raymond Chandler	1944
Isle of the Dead	Ardel Wray, Josef Mischel	1945
Story of GI Joe	Leopold Atlas, Guy Endore, Philip Stevenson	1945
A Tree Grows in Brooklyn	Tess Slesinger, Frank Davis	1945
Beauty and the Beast	Jean Cocteau	1946
A Foreign Affair	Charles Brackett, Billy Wilder, Richard L. Breen	1948
1930s		
Son of Frankenstein	Willis Cooper	1939
His Girl Friday	Charles Lederer, Ben Hecht, Charles MacArthur	1940
Lost Horizon	Robert Riskin	1937
Vampyr	Christen Jul, Carl Theodor Dreyer	1932
Grand Hotel	Vicki Baum, William Absalom Drake, Bela Balazs	1932
1950s		
Stalag 17	Billy Wilder, Edwin Blum, Donald Bevan	1953
Others		
Schlinder's List	Steven Zallian, Thomas Keneally	1993
Gutenberg Books		
Strange Case of Dr. Jekeyl and Mr. Hyde	Robert Louis Stevenson	1886
The Brothers Karamazov	Fyodor Dostoevsky	1880
Thus Spoke Zarathustra	Friedrich Nietzsche/Translated by Thomas Common	1883–1885
The Golden Wheel Dream Book and Fortune Teller	Felix Fontaine	1862
Frankenstein	Mary Shelley	1818
Dracula	Bram Stoker	1897
The Return of Tarzan	Edgar Rice Burroughs	1913
The AntiChrist	Friedrich Nietzsche	1888/1895
The Monster Men	Edgar Rice Burroughs	1913
On War	Carl von Clausewitz	1832
Famous Modern Ghost Stories	Dorothy Scarborough, Ed.	1921

(*Continued*)

Table 4.1 (Continued)

Movies/Book Year	Author	Year
Human, All Too Human	Friedrich Nietzsche	1878
Venus in Furs	Leopold Sacher-Masoch	1870
Memories: A Story of German Love	F. Max Muller	1903
Falling in Love	Grant Allen	1889
Beyond Good and Evil	Friedrich Nietzsche	1886
Applied Eugenics	Paul Popenoe, Roswell Hill Johnson	1921
The Witch Cult in Western Europe	Margaret Alice Murray	1921
Crime: Its Cause and Treatment	Clarence Darrow	1922
Studies in the Psychology of Sex, Volume 3: Analysis of the Sexual Impulse	Havelock Ellis	1901
Studies in the Psychology of Sex, Volume 4: Sexual Selection in Man	Havelock Ellis	1905
Studies in the Psychology of Sex, Volume 6: Sex in Relation to Society	Havelock Ellis	1920
Three Contributions to the Theory of Sex	Sigmund Freud	1905
The Journal of Abnormal Psychology Volume 10	Morton Prince, Ed	1915
The Witch-Cult in Western Europe: A Study in Anthropology	Margaret Alice Murray	1921
Animal Castration	Alexandre Francois Augustin Liautard	1902
The Criminal	Havelock Ellis	1890
Essays in Wartime—Further Studies in the Task of Social Hygiene	Havelock Ellis	1917

century to the mid-1940s. These texts were chosen to create a historical and geographic sense of the characters that the opera was based on.

Working with software developers it took a few months to create the right balance so AIBO would produce coherent answers that were not gibberish and did not repeat. The following are samples from four different tests using variations in temperature as well as different version numbers, meaning the number version the developers used. The default value in the modulating temperature is 1, and the floating point, if started at 0, uses the highest probability for a match. If the temperature is increased, then there is a lower probability of a predictive sentence and more randomness. There is no practical limit to the numbers that can be used in a temperature variable, but I found the variations in responses increase wildly from the integers 3 to 4. When the temperature was increased it gave more weight

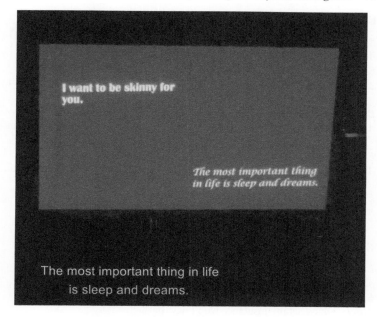

Figure 4.3 Overhead screen displaying live time - upper left Eva's libretto, right AIBO's response, bottom left text to speech interpretation that the audience hears

to other words in the predictive model. The default temperature for AIBO that worked best during the performance was between 1.1 and 1.2. It is astonishing that in test Example 1 AIBO already identifies with Nazis, without any prompts about that subject at all or any definitions built into the character in advance, or any leading questions from Eva's dialogue. It also uses film scripting cues in parenthesis, a problem that was changed by changing the temperature and having the developers write a short script that did not allow these types of cues. In test Example 2 the model stated a particular phrase or phrase combination referring to the word "Okay." In test Example 3 AIBO seems a little silly but quickly changes tone and begins discussing execution ceremonies. In test Example 4 AIBO is still a little silly and a little drunk but shifts gears to discuss fellow prisoners on death row. Nowhere was a prompt about jail or crime given on Eva's side. During the actual performance of the opera all AIBO's responses were unique and randomly generated live time in the Google cloud. All of Eva's statements were scripted in advance but generated in random order for the performer to verbalize.

Example 1—Temperature 1, Version 2.2

EVA: I was given my first camera at age 13.

AIBO: (to child) That's right there.

EVA: The photo store I worked in was only 20 minutes from my home.

AIBO: (fading in) (to child) Now you know a lot about the old Nazis, don't you?

EVA: I was a junior assistant in the studio and darkroom.

AIBO: Darkroom—the barn with the slats—I can see how that ended up in your picture.

EVA: I typed, filled in invoices, and modeled in the photo studio.

AIBO: (to child) Why are you so interested in me when you're supposed to stop?

EVA: My boss took photos of powerful men.

AIBO: (to child) Then you know a lot about what went on in my factory.

Example 2—Temperature 1.5, Version 2.2

EVA: I was given my first camera at age 13.

AIBO: Okay.

EVA: The photo store I worked in was only 20 minutes from my home.

AIBO: Okay, but my insurance won't pay for this.

EVA: I was a junior assistant in the studio and darkroom.

AIBO: Okay.

EVA: I typed, filled in invoices, and modeled in the photo studio.

AIBO: And your parents know full well a very little part in Howey's journalism, which I thought was the finest of any company I ever hired.

EVA: My boss took photos of powerful men.

AIBO: Okay!

Example 3—Temperature 2, Version 2.2

EVA: I was given my first camera at age 13.

AIBO: How old am I, old as fourteen; but I'll forgive you.

EVA: The photo store I worked in was only 20 minutes from my home.

AIBO: What about me.

EVA: I was a junior assistant in the studio and darkroom.

AIBO: Does not apply to you—that means you did not even eat any fruits and processed any junk food, until we checked.

EVA: I typed, filled in invoices, and modeled in the photo studio.

AIBO: Did you like him too I asked you as a child?

EVA: My boss took photos of powerful men.

AIBO: What was his name, his social name he always used to have execution ceremonies.

Example 4—Temperature 3, Version 2.2

EVA: I was given my first camera at age 13.

AIBO: We do a special trick, and you shoot over here from below with no glass. To go, say, four times up onto Lido.

EVA: The photo store I worked in was only 20 minutes from my home.

AIBO: And what did these two fellow prisoners on death row have for picnic supper?

EVA: I was a junior assistant in the studio and darkroom.

AIBO: Darkroom!

EVA: I typed, filled in invoices, and modeled in the photo studio.

AIBO: Didn't know much about pictures then.

EVA: My boss took photos of powerful men.

AIBO: Prafuling and shouting orders did Mr. Praemer.

Sentiment Analysis

The issue of how to classify phenomenologically experienced emotions is complicated and fraught with subjectivity (Nummenmaa et al., 2018; Maas et al., 2011). It is not the purpose of this chapter to delve into the fascinating and extensive arguments in this field but just to work with the simplest analysis that the Google cloud returned. The scores of AIBO's responses to Eva's dialogue were based on an analysis of affective states and subjective information. They returned three viable indicators: "neg" or negative, "neu" or neutral, and "pos" or positive. Two additional viable indicators of high positive and high negative, though available, were not used in order to streamline the signal processing lag time during the performance. These scores were calculated as soon as AIBO returned a text-to-speech response. They were analyzed in the Google cloud using NLP. When the sentiment was analyzed and a corresponding emotional valued matched, the DMX lighting in the black box theater suffused a corner of the room with a different colored light: red for negative, green for positive and yellow for neutral. AIBO also tried, but failed, to reconstruct the last emotionally themed projected memory Eva had launched from her EEG-enabled brainwave headset. AIBO wanted to learn from Eva how to experience a human emotional memory, but since AIBO was only a GPT-2 constructed entity it could never really learn how to have an authentic emotional memory. The videos AIBO hijacked from Eva's previous "memories" were processed through Max/MSP Jitter to give them a "glitchy" unfinished and distorted look.

While interacting with AIBO Eva was experiencing and displaying four emotions related to her EEG brainwave headset: interest, excitement, meditation and frustration. Her emotions lit up on her bodysuit of light while they simultaneously triggered emotionally themed videos and an emotionally themed sonic environment. Her emotions did not all arise simultaneously, but when they reached a certain predetermined threshold they glowed on a

Figure 4.4 A glitchy image of Eva's last negative memory that AIBO tries but fails to imitate

Source: Photo by Taavet Jansen

specially constructed smart textile costume dress. The emotions and colors were yellow for excitement, lavender for interest, red for frustration and green for meditation. Four overhead screens also projected the videos of her emotional states when they were triggered. Contextualized in terms of the entire performance of ABIO, the GPT-2 database deployment was just one part of the entire experience. This chapter does not focus on the brain computer interface, the smart textiles costume, or the triggering of videos and audio by Eva, except as they relate to her interaction with the GPT-2 AI character AIBO.

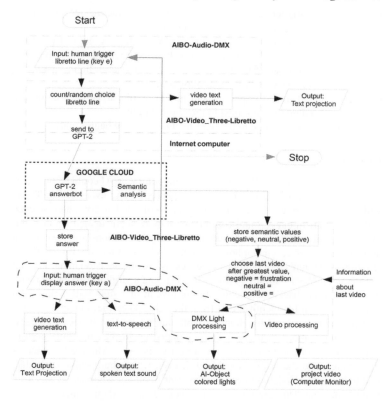

Figure 4.5 Technical diagram of the specific routing of GPT-2, Eva and the performance

Source: Diagram by Hans Gunter Lock

The signal routing and information flow for the GPT-2 AI were as follows:

- Eva speaks a line from the libretto taken from the biography of Eva von Braun.
- The libretto is displayed as text on an overhead screen in yellow letters.
- The same libretto text is sent to the GPT-2 in the cloud.
- The libretto text receives a response from the GPT-2 also conveyed as text.
- The text is displayed on an overhead screen as blue letters.
- The blue text from the GPT-2 is converted to synthesized speech that the audience is able to hear.
- The blue text is simultaneously analyzed in the cloud for emotional senti-ment content—either positive, negative or neutral.

- The analysis triggers a colored light in a corner of the theater: positive is green, negative is red, and yellow is neutral.
- The sentiment analysis also triggers a video reflecting the last positive, negative or neutral emotional memory Eva experienced while speaking the libretto and wearing her EEG headset and bodysuit of light. That video corresponds to AIBO's current emotional state.
- The sentiment image imperfect and glitchy is displayed on a computer screen placed on the floor next to the colored lights.
- Eva speaks the next line in the libretto, and the cycle begins anew.

Discussion

The opera was created to illustrate one salient point—an AI could be built (for artistic purposes) to be twisted, neurotic, perverted and even fascist. Those with much strong computer programming skills and a computer science and mathematical background could make a more sophisticated version, but I most certainly obtained my objective. The story, or relationship between Eva and AIBO, serves as a metaphor for humankind's infatuation with AI. While reading von Braun's biography I was struck by the one decision in her life that forever defined her—falling in love. How is it that a virginal 17-year-old with a strict Catholic background could fall in love at first sight with a man who lied to her about his identity right from the start? They met in October 1929 at a photo shop owned by Heinrich Hoffman, where Eva was employed as a clerk and a photo assistant. Adolph stopped by to pick up some portrait photos Hoffman had taken of him telling Eva he was "Mr. Wolf." None of that mattered to the impressionable girl, even when she discovered he had lied to her. She was determined to marry "Mr. Wolf" or whoever he was from that moment on. This combination of naivete, denial and ignorance enabled a monster. Her selection of "Mr. Wolf" metaphorically parallels systems being put in place that cede control of many basic forms of human congress over to AI. It is not my purpose to list all the ways this is occurring, as they are rapidly changing depending on who or what is behind their development. My purpose is to bring attention to the misjudgment, misunderstanding, total belief in, and overdependence on AI en masse. I am not against AI and am aware of the many important and wonderful things it can accomplish, but it is precisely this overconfidence I find deeply troubling. Discussing these aspects with coders and developers can be but is not always frustrating. Many developers think mathematics is inherently unbiased, and algorithms are incapable of doing or promoting harm. Even if an algorithmic process is shown to be biased or incapable of making truly correct decisions many private and/or governmental systems have them in place. When these systems are launched, there is often no accountability. Reasons of national security are citied, or the end product is private and protected by intellectual property law. This places anyone who is the target of these systems or even an innocent bystander in a precarious position. There is nowhere to turn, and no one to turn to concerning corrective measures, compensation or redressing about the actions and mistakes an AI-driven system could take.

Recently some developers have insisted that AI systems are already sentient, such as the controversy around Google's LaMDA chatbot (Kilcher, 2022). This approach removes responsibility for the prompt engineering, programming and response of the chatbot and its developers placing it onto the questions input by the user. It introduces a system that can be overwritten by different organizations, governments, corporations or other large and well-resourced entities to be restrictive. There are also open innovation large language models (LLM) such as BLOOM that have implicit ethical considerations. Because they are maintained and reviewed by communities of developers and programmers (Bloom RAIL License v. 1.0, 2022), enforcement of their terms and conditions will most likely spawn a new generation of intellectual property lawyers and international court trials. It is beyond the scope of this chapter to discuss the legal and other issues these specific technologies could raise.

Conclusion

AI agents have increased in strength, especially since the introduction in February 2019 of the powerful GPT-2 algorithm created by OpenAI. In the emotionally intelligent AIBO, the GPT-2 algorithm was built to be a "sicko" or perverted character. This was done through the process of "overfitting" or using an overly narrow scope to draw attention to the potential misuses of AI. The character was seeded with 47 copyright-free preselected texts about monsters, human dysfunction and books about power and dominance, among others. The texts were situated in the time frame from the late 1800s until the 1940s. A basic emotional semantic analysis on AIBO's GPT-2 responses to Eva's libretto was undertaken using NLP. The point of this was to analyze the synthetic emotions of a synthetic being as if they were real emotions.

This combination of performance practices and data manipulation served a number of purposes in terms of the GPT-2 character. It demonstrated the relative ease with which an AI can be developed that is not in alignment with expected human norms. It wondered if building a "sicko" AI was possible, which was demonstrated to be true. It also considered the implications of deploying AI agents in society at large and using their algorithmic thinking to shape critical decisions regarding wide swaths of human congress. It questions if human feelings and conditions are being distilled to over quantified responses, often without third-party recourse. The opera also considers the relationship between brain computer interfaces, the human animal, AI, biometrics and contemplates on their speculative and intertwined futures.

82 *Ellen Pearlman*

Acknowledgments—Vertigo STARTS, GoProSocial, ThoughtWorks Arts, Jonathan Heng, W. Somo, Hans Gunter Lock, Dila Denmir, Sniedze Strauta.

References

Bloom RAIL License v.1.0—A Hugging Face Space by BigScience. (2022, May 19). *Hugging face—the AI community building the future.* http://huggingface.co/spaces/bigscience/license

Brown, T. B., Benjamin, B., Ryder, N., et al. (2020, July 22). *Language models are few-shot learners.* arXiv.org. https://ariv.org/abs/2005.14165

Heikkila, M. (2022, July 12). Inside a radical new project to democratize AI. *MIT Technology Review.* hppts://www.technologyreview.com/2022/07/12/1055817/inside-a-radical-new-project-to-democratize-ai/

Kilcher, Y. (2022, June 15). Did Google's LaMDA chatbot just become sentient? *YouTube.* www.youtube.com/watch?v=mIZLGBD99iU

Kline, A. S. (2000). *Ovid (43BC-17)—The metamorphoses: Book 10.* Poetry in Translation, A. S. Kline's Open Access Poetry Archive. www.poetryintranslation.com/PITBR/Latin/Metamorph10.php#anchor_Toc64105570

Lambert, A. (2014). *The lost life of Eva Braun: A biography.* St. Martin's Press.

Maas, A. L., Daly, R. E., Pham, P., Tl et al. (2011, June). Learning word vectors for sentiment analysis. *ACL Anthology.* https://aclanthology.org/P11-1015/

Nummenmaa, L., Riita, H., Jari, H. K., Glerean, E., et al. (2018, August 28). *Maps of subjective feelings.* www.pnas.org/doi/full/10.1073/pnas.1807390115. https://doi.org/10.1073/pnas.1807390115

OpenAI, *Unsupervised Sentiment Neuron.* (2020, October 5). *OpenAI.* https://openai.com/blog/unsupervised-sentiment-neuron/

OpenAI, *Better Language Models and Their Implications.* (2021, June 21). *OpenAI.* hppts://openai.com/blog/better-language-models/

Software. (n.d.). *The Stanford natural language processing group.* https://nlp.stanford.edu/software/

Weizenbaum. (1966). Eliza a computer program for the study of natural language communication between man and machine. *Communications of the ACD, 9,* 36–45.

Index

Rousseff, Dilma (impeachment trial) 10
Rumble videos 19–21; profile mentions, network *21*

Salvini, Matteo 13–14
Sánchez-Olmos, Cande 46, 66
Saturday Night Live (TV show) 51
science work, perception 6–7
Selfish Gene, The (Dawkins) 47
sentiment analysis 77–80; analysis 70
Shapiro, Ben 5–6
shareworthiness, fake news (relationship) 53–56
sharing 46; disinformation sharing 30–31; fake news sharing 5
Shaw, Bernard 69
sicko GPT-2 AIBO character, development 69–70
Snopes, debunking 55
social anxiety, manifestations (increase) 3
social media: algorithms, usage 31–32; disinformation, increase 8; fake news, avoidance (impossibility) 54; opinion leaders, role 9; pervasiveness 3; role 4–7
social, multivocality 25
social network analysis (SNA) 12; application 12–13
social networks, establishment 9
social platforms, emergence 9
source: reputation 9; types (analysis), TCAT (usage) 12–13
source-based methods, usage 35
Spears, Britney 49
Speel, Hans-Cees 48
Strauta, Sniedze 72
style-based methods, usage 352
Sunstein, Cass 9
supergreen pass, data collection 10
Swift, Taylor 48

TCAT, usage 12
Telegram (closed nature) 53–54
TikTok, political content (engagement) 6

tragedy 52
transmedia 58
Trump, Donald: campaign victory/election 2, 4; chloroquine/hydroxychloroquine benefits, transmission 3; pandemic effects minimization 7; Pope Francis support, hoax 56
Tumblr, fake quotes (generation) 59
Twitter: analysis methodologies 10–22; bots 32; data analysis, results 13–19; data collection 10; dataset, profiles (dominance) *13*; discussion peaks *11*; echo chambers, phenomenon 10; feeds 51–52; network analysis *14–17*; online platform 36; opinion leaders, role 8–10; political content, engagement 6; posts 4; social platform, disinformation campaign 2
two-stage communication model 8–9
two-stage flow process 9

uncivil discussions 36
unintentional mistakes, impact 30–31
unverified information, dissemination (curbing) 6

virality, impact 56
visibility, increase 2
von Braun, Eva 71–72, 80

war refugees (description), negative image (trigger) *71*
"Weekend Update, The" 51
Weizenbaum, Joseph 69
WhatsApp (closed nature) 53–54
West, Kanye 48

YouTube: channels 19; examples 33; links/videos 12; online platform 36; social platform, disinformation campaign 2

zero-shot settings 72
zombie deer virus outbreak, hoax 57